CAMPAIGN • 221

THE FIRST BATTLE OF THE MARNE 1914

The French 'miracle' halts the Germans

IAN SUMNER　　　ILLUSTRATED BY GRAHAM TURNER

Series editor Marcus Cowper

First published in Great Britain in 2010 by Osprey Publishing,
Midland House, West Way, Botley, Oxford OX2 0PH, UK
44-02 23rd St, Suite 219, Long Island City, NY 11101, USA
E-mail: info@ospreypublishing.com

A CIP catalogue record for this book is available from the British Library.

ISBN: 978 1 84603 502 9
E book ISBN: 978 1 84908 270 9

Editorial by Ilios Publishing Ltd, Oxford, UK (www.iliospublishing.com)
Page layout by: The Black Spot
Index by Margaret Vaudrey
Typeset in Myriad Pro and Sabon
Maps by Bounford.com
3D bird's-eye views by The Black Spot
Battlescene illustrations by Graham Turner
Originated by PPS Grasmere Ltd
Printed in China through Worldprint Ltd.

09 10 11 12 13   10 9 8 7 6 5 4 3 2 1

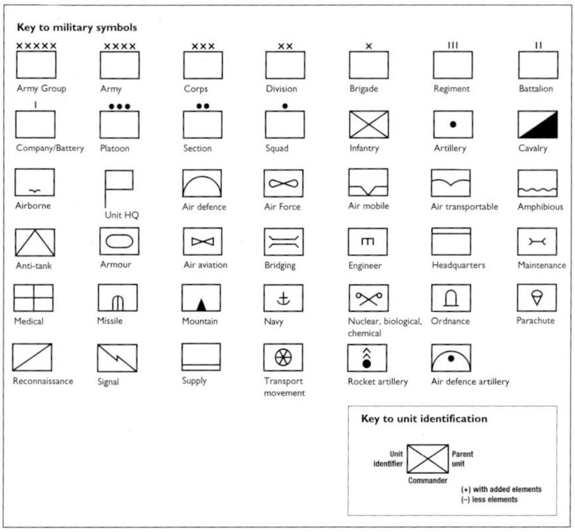

ACKNOWLEDGEMENTS

I am grateful to everyone who has helped in the preparation of this book,
particularly my wife Maggie for services above and beyond (as usual),
Katherine Bracewell, Jack Sheldon, the staffs of the municipal library at
Meaux, East Riding Libraries and of the Service Historique de la Défense
at Vincennes. All the illustrations are from the author's collection.

ARTIST'S NOTE

Readers may care to note that the original paintings from which the
colour plates in this book were prepared are available for private sale.
The Publishers retain all reproduction copyright whatsoever.
All enquiries should be addressed to:

Graham Turner, PO Box 568, Aylesbury, Buckinghamshire, HP17 8ZK, UK

The Publishers regret that they can enter into no correspondence upon
this matter.

THE WOODLAND TRUST

Osprey Publishing are supporting the Woodland Trust, the UK's leading
woodland conservation charity, by funding the dedication of trees.

Key to military symbols

XXXXX	XXXX	XXX	XX	X	III	II
Army Group	Army	Corps	Division	Brigade	Regiment	Battalion
I	●●●	●●	●			
Company/Battery	Platoon	Section	Squad	Infantry	Artillery	Cavalry
Airborne	Unit HQ	Air defence	Air Force	Air mobile	Air transportable	Amphibious
Anti-tank	Armour	Air aviation	Bridging	Engineer	Headquarters	Maintenance
Medical	Missile	Mountain	Navy	Nuclear, biological, chemical	Ordnance	Parachute
Reconnaissance	Signal	Supply	Transport movement	Rocket artillery	Air defence artillery	

Key to unit identification

Unit Identifier		Parent unit
	Commander	

(+) with added elements
(–) less elements

FOR A CATALOGUE OF ALL BOOKS PUBLISHED BY OSPREY MILITARY
AND AVIATION PLEASE CONTACT:

NORTH AMERICA
Osprey Direct, c/o Random House Distribution Center, 400 Hahn
Road, Westminster, MD 21157
E-mail: info@ospreydirect.com

ALL OTHER REGIONS
Osprey Direct, The Book Service Ltd, Distribution Centre, Colchester
Road, Frating Green, Colchester, Essex, CO7 7DW
E-mail: customerservice@ospreypublishing.com

www.ospreypublishing.com

CONTENTS

The German march to the Marne, 15 August–5 September 1914

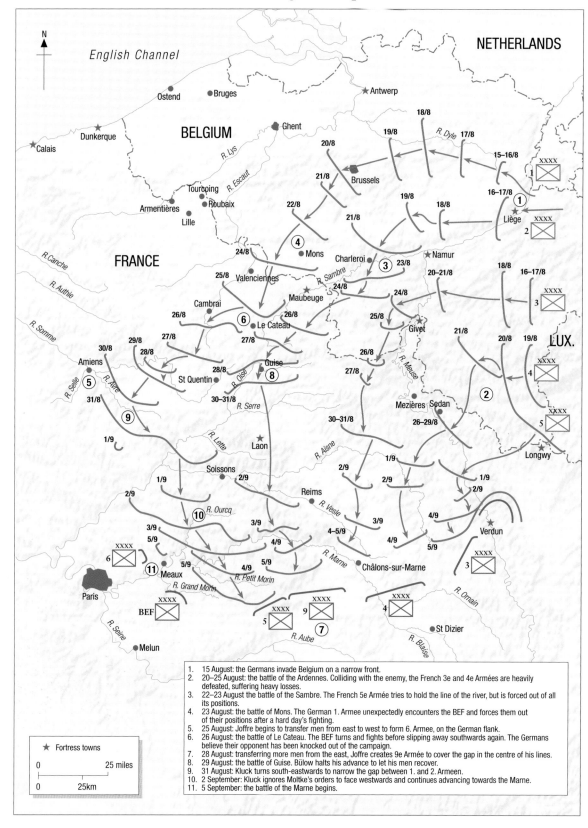

N

English Channel

NETHERLANDS

Ostend • Bruges
★ Antwerp
Calais ★
Dunkerque
BELGIUM
• Ghent
R. Lys
R. Dyle
18/8
19/8   17/8
15–16/8
XXXX
1
16–17/8
Tourcoing
R. Escaut
20/8
21/8
Brussels
1
Roubaix
Armentières
Lille
22/8
19/8
18/8
Liège ★
XXXX
2
21/8
FRANCE
R. Canche
24/8
④
• Mons
Charleroi
③ 23/8
★ Namur
20–21/8
18/8
16–17/8
XXXX
3
R. Authie
25/8 Valenciennes
R. Sambre
24/8
24/8
18/8
20/8
19/8
LUX.
Cambrai
26/8
Maubeuge
25/8
Givet
21/8
R. Somme
30/8
29/8
27/8
⑥ Le Cateau
27/8
26/8
R. Meuse
XXXX
4
Amiens
28/8
26/8
27/8
20/8
R. Selle
⑤
St Quentin
28/8
Guise
R. Oise
⑧
Mézières   Sedan
26–29/8
XXXX
5
31/8
30–31/8
R. Serre
30–31/8
Longwy ★
⑨
R. Lette
Laon ★
1/9
R. Aisne
1/9
Verdun ★
2/9
Soissons
2/9
2/9
⑩ R. Ourcq
Reims
R. Vesle
2/9
1/9
2/9
XXXX
3
1/9
3/9
3/9
4/9
4–5/9
3/9
4/9
Paris
5/9
4/9
5/9
5/9
R. Seine
XXXX
6
⑪ Meaux
5/9
4/9
5/9
Châlons-sur-Marne
R. Marne
R. Ornain
R. Grand Morin
R. Petit Morin
XXXX
4
• Melun
XXXX
BEF
XXXX
5
XXXX
9
⑦
R. Aube
• St Dizier
R. Blaise

★ Fortress towns

0 _____ 25 miles
0 _____ 25km

1. 15 August: the Germans invade Belgium on a narrow front.
2. 20–25 August: the battle of the Ardennes. Colliding with the enemy, the French 3e and 4e Armées are heavily defeated, suffering heavy losses.
3. 22–23 August the battle of the Sambre. The French 5e Armée tries to hold the line of the river, but is forced out of all its positions.
4. 23 August: the battle of Mons. The German 1. Armee unexpectedly encounters the BEF and forces them out of their positions after a hard day's fighting.
5. 25 August: Joffre begins to transfer men from east to west to form 6. Armee, on the German flank.
6. 26 August: the battle of Le Cateau. The BEF turns and fights before slipping away southwards again. The Germans believe their opponent has been knocked out of the campaign.
7. 28 August: transferring more men from the east, Joffre creates 9e Armée to cover the gap in the centre of his lines.
8. 29 August: the battle of Guise. Bülow halts his advance to let his men recover.
9. 31 August: Kluck turns south-eastwards to narrow the gap between 1. and 2. Armeen.
10. 2 September: Kluck ignores Moltke's orders to face westwards and continues advancing towards the Marne.
11. 5 September: the battle of the Marne begins.

OPENING MOVES

On the opening of hostilities in August 1914 both sides were counting on a short war. For Alfred Graf von Schlieffen, writing some years earlier as Chief of the Großer Generalstab (German General Staff), the initial battles were likely to be crucial. They would decide any future conflict because of the 'pacifist tendencies of the majority of the European people'. French field service regulations embodied similar ideas: 'The nature of the war, the size of the forces involved, the difficulties of resupplying them, the interruption of the social and economic life of the nation, all encourage the search for a decision in the shortest possible time to end the fighting quickly.' Such thinking determined French and German war plans. Both parties aimed simply to put the maximum number of men into uniform as quickly as they could.

French actions followed Plan XVII, which became effective in May 1914. This was not primarily an operational war plan. Instead it focused on the mobilization, concentration and deployment of French forces. Four armies were assembled along the Belgian, Luxembourg and German frontiers, while a fifth was held in reserve. And the disposition of these armies – in a central position – was flexible enough for them to strike in a number of directions.

However, a number of constraints served to limit this freedom of action. Politically, France had no option but to take the offensive – both to free the 'lost' provinces of Alsace and Lorraine, and to fulfil its treaty obligations. (The Franco-Russian treaties guaranteed a French attack 11 days after mobilization.)

French troops on the march. In the weeks preceding the battle, a daily march of more than 20km (12 miles) was not unusual, particularly for formations on the outside of the wheeling German line of march.

French infantrymen defending the line of a hedgerow. Even in action, they are still wearing their packs. During the battles of the Frontiers, the sun reflecting off their highly polished mess tins revealed more French positions than their red trousers ever did.

At the same time it was equally important that France preserve Belgian neutrality. Joffre knew a German attack was most likely to come through Belgium. But on no account could he cross the border to pre-empt it. A succession of pre-war joint staff meetings had failed to reassure the French that Britain would take part in any land war. Invading Belgium might be all that was needed to provoke Britain into withdrawing its much-needed support.

While Joffre suspected a drive through Belgium, he had no detailed knowledge of German plans, and little idea of the exact size and strength of the forces he faced. Crucially, his experience of French reserve units led him to underestimate the capabilities of their German counterparts. The French Army was reluctant to place its own reserve units in the front line. Pre-war opportunities to keep these units up to a full pitch of training and readiness had been few, and it was feared the reserves would be unable to stand up to the stress of combat. Joffre assumed this also held true for his enemy and calculated that the Germans had insufficient troops to mount a strong attack through Belgium. Their main effort would therefore have to come further south. Even when French intelligence services provided a complete German order of battle, Joffre remained unmoved. Noting the lower establishments of German reserve divisions, particularly in artillery, he concluded that these formations were not intended to play a full part in battle.

But Joffre was wrong; the scale of Germany's ambitions meant that its reserve formations would play a key role from the outset. In contrast to their opponents, the German reserves had benefited from regular periods of peacetime training and their performance in combat would more than justify the decision to include them in the front line. With plenty of men available, the Germans had ample resources to mount their main attack through Belgium.

The German plan followed ideas outlined by Schlieffen in a memorandum of 1906, which suggested an advance through Belgium as a means of circumventing the formidable obstacle presented by the line of fortresses defending the Franco-German frontier. Indeed, to bypass the great frontier redoubt of Liège, Schlieffen was even prepared to invade the Netherlands. Pinning the French right in its fortresses along the Meuse, the Germans would first advance in a great curve through Belgium and northern France. Then sweeping around Paris they would go on to roll up the French armies and crush them against the Swiss frontier. Key to the plan was speed. The

Germans were seeking at all costs to avoid a war on two fronts. They judged that the French would be quicker into the field than their Russian allies, so it would be vital to deal them a knockout blow first before turning to meet the threat from the east.

Schlieffen's successor, Moltke, accepted the strategic assumptions behind the plan, but made several important revisions. Firstly he abandoned the invasion of the Netherlands, judged politically unwise. This had a dual effect – forcing the German right to advance on a restricted front across the short Belgo-German frontier and making it important to capture Liège as quickly as possible. Then, anticipating that France would make the first move by invading Alsace and Lorraine, Moltke acted to bolster the defence of the disputed provinces by transferring troops from his right to his left.

International tension was growing during the summer of 1914. On 1 August France issued its mobilization orders. But, anxious not to appear the aggressor, its commanders were ordered not to encroach within 10km (6 miles) of the Franco-German border. The following day small parties of German soldiers crossed that frontier and on 3 August Germany formally declared war on France. Then on 4 August German troops crossed over into Belgium – finally provoking Great Britain into declaring war on Germany.

On 8 August Joffre revealed his strategic plan. A small force would advance into Alsace; 1ère and 2e Armées would advance into Lorraine, south of the fortifications of Metz-Thionville; 3e and 4e Armées would advance north of Metz-Thionville into Belgium and Luxembourg; finally, 5e Armée would cover the left flank in Belgium. Joffre's intentions were to pin the enemy left in Alsace, then go on to rupture the centre, so leaving the right isolated in Belgium.

The advance of 1ère and 2e Armées first slowed and then stopped in the face of German resistance and difficult going in hilly, wooded countryside. The two French armies were advancing on divergent paths – becoming progressively weaker as they moved forwards – and the Germans were able to defeat them in detail. On 21 August Joffre ordered a partial withdrawal,

French infantry advancing. This is almost certainly a pre-war shot. But given the relatively close order demonstrated here it is unsurprising that casualties were so heavy.

A German column passing through Brussels. The garrison of captured towns was left to ersatz formations. The security of his long right flank through Belgium caused Moltke constant concern.

a move that suited his overall plan because it drew in the German left. The German right, meanwhile, appeared stronger than had first been anticipated. Paradoxically, Joffre took heart from this. He reasoned that the Germans must have weakened their centre, so making it ripe for his decisive thrust.

The following day 3e and 4e Armées collided with 4. and 5. Armeen in the Ardennes. With little idea of German positions or strength, the French were heavily defeated in a series of meeting engagements.

In fact, the Germans were present in far greater strength than expected all along the line, although it still took some time for Joffre to recognize this. On the French left, 5e Armée was spread out, trying to cover a front of 100km (60 miles) along the rivers Meuse and Sambre. Clashes took place between opposing cavalry forces. But the performance of the French did not impress. Sordet's Corps de cavalerie lost one-sixth of its personnel, but reportedly did not sustain 'a single wound from a sabre'. On 21 August advance units of 2. Armee had crossed the Sambre and driven back 5e Armée. Caught by surprise, nothing the French tried over the next two days could secure the crossings and they were eventually forced away from the river line. At the same time, the men of the newly arrived British Expeditionary Force (BEF) took up their place on the left of 5e Armée around the town of Mons. But they too were eventually forced from their positions.

With the battles of the Frontiers, Joffre's offensive had failed. He had grossly underestimated enemy capabilities – the German reserves had shown that they were more than capable of holding their own – and had dispersed his offensive strength by sending his armies in three different directions.

CHRONOLOGY

1914

3 August Germany declares war on France and invades Belgium. Britain declares war on Germany.

12 August The BEF begins to arrive in France under the command of Sir John French. French is told that he must on no account consider himself under Joffre's orders.

14–23 August Battles of the Frontiers: advancing into the Ardennes, the French are defeated with heavy losses and begin to retreat.

16 August The Germans secure the last of the Liège forts.

17 August 1. and 2. Armeen continue their advance through Belgium. Sir John French meets with Lanrezac, commander of 5e Armée. The result is mutual suspicion and dislike.

23 August The battle of Mons: the BEF temporarily checks the advance of 1. Armee (Kluck), inflicting heavy casualties. Nevertheless, the German advance continues.

24 August On the French left Joffre orders a retreat in the face of the German advance.

25 August Joffre begins to assemble a new 6e Armée (Maunoury) – created by transferring troops from Alsace and Lorraine – on the far left of the Allied line. As far as Sir John French is concerned, the French Army is a beaten force.

26 August The battle of Le Cateau: Kluck is briefly checked by II Corps in hard fighting. But he still views the battle as a defeat for the BEF. So too do the French. Their liaison officer reports to GQG (Grand Quartier Général – French Supreme Headquarters) that the British have been crushed.

27 August An official OHL (Oberste Heeresleitung – German Supreme Headquarters) communiqué describes the Allied armies as '… in full retreat [and] incapable of offering serious resistance to the German advance…'. Moltke orders his right wing to carry on moving south-west. Meanwhile 6. Armee (Kronprinz Rupprecht of Bavaria) and 7e Armée (Heeringen) will attack on the Moselle between Toul and Epinal.

28 August Joffre creates another new formation, later designated 9e Armée (Foch).

29 August Battle of Guise: 5e Armée (Lanrezac) attacks and badly mauls 2. Armee (Bülow).

30 August The main thrust of the German attack has been pulled south/south-east. Confident that 5e Armée and the BEF have been defeated, Moltke orders

Kluck and Bülow to abandon the attack on Paris and turn south-east to close up with 3. Armee (Hausen).

31 August Kluck begins his turn. His move is spotted by Allied reconnaissance and the first reports reach Joffre. But GQG does not immediately spot the opportunity for a counteroffensive.

1 September 1. Armee comes within 48km (30 miles) of Paris. Reports continue to filter through to GQG. But it is not until 3 September that the crucial change in direction is finally confirmed by Allied intelligence.

2 September Moltke orders 1. Armee to place itself in echelon behind 2. Armee to provide cover for the open German right flank. But Kluck ignores these instructions and continues his rapid advance.

3 September 1. Armee reaches the Marne, but its right flank is now exposed. Général de division Gallieni, the military governor of Paris, makes plans to attack. Joffre sacks the pessimistic Lanrezac and appoints Général de division Franchet d'Esperey in his place.

4 September 1. Armee continues across the Marne. Joffre commits to a general counteroffensive to begin on 7 September but learns that Sir John French is reluctant to get involved.

5 September Battle of the Ourcq: rear elements of Kluck's right flank still remain north of the Marne. Advancing east towards the Ourcq, 6e Armée collides with them north of Meaux.

Battle of the two Morins: confronted by Joffre, Sir John French finally agrees to join the counteroffensive. Advance elements of 1. Armee reach the Villiers-Saint-Georges area, a few kilometres north of the Seine. This is as far as the Germans will penetrate into France.

6 September Battle of the Ourcq: 6e Armée makes some initial gains but 1. Armee holds its ground. Kluck skilfully transfers two corps back across the Marne to bolster his right flank.

Battle of the Saint-Gond marshes: 9e Armée is heavily engaged from Sézanne to Vitry-le-François and is pushed back south of the marshes.

Battle of the two Morins: the BEF moves north towards the Grand Morin.

7 September Battle of the Ourcq: commandeered to transport troops from Paris, 600 taxi cabs help to restore the northern flank of 6e Armée. Kluck still has two corps remaining south of the Marne. He transfers them northwards to the Ourcq – but the move widens the gap between 1. and 2. Armeen.

Battle of the Saint-Gond marshes: attempting to break the Allied centre, 2. and 3. Armeen mount powerful attacks against 9e and 4e Armées (Langle de Cary).

Battle of the two Morins: the BEF and elements of 5e Armée advance slowly, meeting little resistance. The BEF reaches the Petit Morin. The right flank of 5e Armée engages in fierce fighting with 2. Armee at Soizy-aux-Bois. Weakened by the withdrawal of Kluck's two corps, Bülow withdraws his right wing behind the Petit Morin.

8 September Battle of the Ourcq: Maunoury tries to turn the German right wing but his attack gets bogged down. The centre takes Etrépilly with heavy losses. 6e Armée has failed to break the German right and must go on the defensive.

Battle of the Saint-Gond marshes: the Gardekorps and Hausen's 3. Armee launch a powerful surprise attack. They drive back the right wing of 9e Armée and take Fère-Champenoise.

The right wing steadies and holds off further attacks, but 9e Armée suffers heavy losses.

Battle of the two Morins: OHL calls in troops from Brussels and Maubeuge to fill the dangerous gap between 1. and 2. Armeen. The left flank of 5e Armée continues its slow advance. The BEF crosses the Petit Morin and reaches the south bank of the Marne. Fearing his right is about to give way, Bülow recommends that 1. and 2. Armeen retreat before it is too late. Franchet d'Esperey succeeds in turning Bülow's right flank.

9 September

Battle of the Ourcq: Kluck orders his hard-pressed centre and left to pull back. But on his right he succeeds in driving back the weakened 6e Armée. Later that day, in response to the overall situation, he orders a general withdrawal.

Battle of the Saint-Gond marshes: 9e Armée is checked at Mondement and Mont Août. Hausen learns that 2. Armee is withdrawing and immediately orders his right wing to follow suit. Even as the German right begins to fall back, Moltke orders attacks by the centre and left to continue.

Battle of the two Morins: British cavalry lead the way across the Marne and by mid-morning the BEF is over in force. However, 5e Armée has to shift right to help the hard-pressed Foch and cannot reinforce the BEF advance.

Meanwhile the German right wing continues to fall back. This movement effectively costs the Germans the battle of the Marne and ends their hopes of a quick victory in the war. But the BEF and 5e Armée have come to a standstill and the Allies lose their chance to break the German line.

10 September

Joffre orders a cautious 'pursuit' of the retreating Germans, and the Allied left advances a few kilometres against little or no resistance. Belatedly realizing the extent of the German retreat, Joffre orders more vigorous action.

11 September

With the whole of the right and centre falling back, the Germans can offer virtually no resistance. However, the troops of the Allied left and centre are exhausted and unable to advance more than a few kilometres through countryside littered with corpses and abandoned equipment. Joffre formally announces the Allied victory.

12 September

German troops begin to occupy prepared positions behind the Aisne. The gap between 1. and 2. Armeen is finally closed.

14 September

Falkenhayn replaces Moltke as Chief of the OHL.

15 September

The Germans are by now dug in behind the Aisne. Joffre orders the Allied armies to end their pursuit and prepare for methodical warfare. Hopes of a swift Allied victory over Germany fade.

OPPOSING COMMANDERS

ALLIED COMMANDERS

The French were led by **Général de division Joseph Joffre** (1852–1931). In peacetime Joffre held the position of vice-président du Conseil Supérieur de la Guerre et généralissime désigné et chef d'état-major général de l'Armée (Vice-President of the Supreme War Council, commander-in-chief designate and Chief of Army General Staff). On the outbreak of war he was appointed as commandant en chef du théâtre des opérations du Nord et du Nord-Est (commander of the French forces in the field, with the official title of Commander in Chief of the Armies of the North and North-East). The command of the army as a whole remained in the hands of the minister of war (no less than 13 in number since 1900).

Joffre had been appointed to his position in 1911. As far as his political masters were concerned he was the least worst candidate. The first choice, Général de division Gallieni, had only two years before retirement and excused himself. The two other contenders both fell foul of political misgivings. Général de division Paul Pau boldly requested the right to choose his own subordinates – too much for politicians forever fearful of an army coup. And Général de division Edouard de Castelnau was simply too Catholic for a government mistrustful of religion of any kind. Gallieni supported the candidacy of the forcefully republican Joffre, who had served under him in Madagascar in 1895.

An engineer, Joffre excelled in the building of railways and had worked on the fortification of France's north-east frontier. He had also served in the Far East and West Africa, as well as Madagascar. But he had made his reputation primarily as a technician and administrator rather than as an operational commander. A man of regular habits, he placed great store on regular meals and a good night's sleep. He went to bed early each night, making it clear he was not to be disturbed under any circumstances. He was neither a great nor an original thinker, but his strength lay in listening to those who were. When a problem was put before him, he took his time and gave it careful consideration. And, once he had made up his mind, his strong will would see the matter through.

On the outset of war Joffre's army commanders were nearly all infantrymen: **Augustin Dubail** (1851–1934), **Edouard de Castelnau** (1841–1944), **Fernand de Langle de Cary** (1849–1927) and **Charles Lanrezac** (1852–1924) commanded 1ère, 2e, 3e and 5e Armées respectively. Artilleryman **Pierre Ruffey**

(1851–1928), who commanded 3e Armée, was the only exception. Joffre went on to create three more armies during the course of the campaign. **Paul Pau** (1848–1932) – another infantryman and the unsuccessful candidate of 1911 – came out of retirement shortly after the declaration of war to command the Armée d'Alsace; artillerymen **Michel Maunoury** (1847–1923) and **Ferdinand Foch** (1851–1929) took control of 6e and 9e Armées respectively. All these men had taken part in the Franco-German War of 1870–71. But only Langle de Cary and Dubail had subsequently seen service outside France.

Pau, Ruffey and Lanrezac were all sacked during the course of the campaign. Pau's Armée d'Alsace was broken up, its troops sent elsewhere. Ruffey was replaced by **Maurice Sarrail** (1856–1929), an infantryman who had seen service in North Africa. Lanrezac was succeeded by **Louis Franchet d'Esperey** (1856–1942) – 'Desperate Frankie' to the British troops – another infantryman and a veteran of North Africa and Indochina.

The forces at Joffre's disposal were augmented by the BEF, commanded by **Field Marshal Sir John French** (1852–1925). French had made his reputation as a cavalry commander during the Boer War. Appointed Chief of the Imperial General Staff in 1912, he had resigned in March 1914 over the Curragh Incident. But he was recalled at the end of July 1914 and appointed Commander-in-Chief of the BEF.

Serving under French were **Lieutenant-General Sir Douglas Haig** (1861–28), who commanded I Corps, and **General Sir Horace Smith-Dorrien** (1858–30), who led II Corps. A third corps, under **Lieutenant-General Sir William Pulteney** (1861–41), was forming at the time of the battle. However, only Major-General Snow's 4th Division and an extra brigade were available in France. The cavalry consisted of one division, commanded by **Major-General Edmund Allenby** (1861–1936), and 'Gough's Command' – three regiments under **Brigadier-General Hubert Gough** (1870–1963).

Smith-Dorrien and Pulteney were infantrymen; Haig and Allenby, cavalrymen. Smith-Dorrien ('Smith-Doreen' to his men) had only recently taken command, following the death of his predecessor, Lieutenant-General Sir James Grierson, on 17 August. Smith-Dorrien was an excellent trainer and reformer. Indeed, his time in the Aldershot Command had helped to lay the foundations for the high standards of the BEF. Pulteney, on the other hand, was the least qualified of all French's subordinates, attending neither Sandhurst nor the Staff College. In 1917 he was characterized by his chief of staff as 'the most completely ignorant general I served during the war and that is saying a lot'.

LEFT
Kaiser Wilhelm II (left) and chief of staff Helmuth von Moltke on pre-war manoeuvres. On 1 August, as the intricately timetabled German mobilization plan sprang into action, the Kaiser suggested the attack on France be halted and all the Army's resources thrown against Russia. Moltke is reported to have had a heart attack.

CENTRE
Generaloberst von Kluck, commander of 1. Armee. Kluck was an energetic commander always seeking the knockout blow: 'If we leave the enemy alone, even though he is completely worn out, he can regroup, regain his freedom of movement and retrieve his offensive spirit. It is still possible to push him back across the Seine and have time for 1. and 2. Armeen to turn to face Paris.'

RIGHT
Generaloberst von Bülow, commander of 2. Armee. Bülow was in no doubt where to place responsibility for the failure to secure a victory on the Marne: 'the withdrawal in broad daylight of III and IX Armeekorps meant victory for the French'.

GERMAN COMMANDERS

The German generals most closely associated with the battle of the Marne were slightly older than their Allied counterparts. In fact, all were veterans of the war against Austria in 1866. **Helmuth Moltke** (1848–1916) was Chief of the OHL and thus commander of all the German armies in the field. Moltke was the nephew of his more celebrated namesake – who, also Chief of the General Staff, had overseen Prussia's crushing defeats of Austria in 1866 and France in 1870. He was appointed in 1906 and had taken over the war plan of his predecessor, Schlieffen. But Moltke's health was poor and he had suffered a heart attack as recently as 1 August.

On the German right, Moltke's army commanders were **Generaloberst Alexander von Kluck** (1846–1934), **Generaloberst Karl von Bülow** (1846–1921), and **Generaloberst Freiherr Max von Hausen** (1846–1922). Kluck commanded 1. Armee, on the right flank. To his left was 2. Armee under Bülow; then came the Saxons of 3. Armee under Hausen. Based on his performance in peacetime manoeuvres, Bülow had the highest pre-war reputation of the three and had been Moltke's rival in 1906. But in the field he showed himself a cautious commander – certainly too cautious for Kluck, a 'thruster', who chafed under the more prudent approaches of Moltke and Bülow. Of more modest origins than his peers, Kluck was the only army commander who had not attended the Kriegsakademie. Hausen, on the other hand, had a distinguished pedigree. He had served as Saxon war minister between 1902 and 1914, and briefly as Saxon prime minister.

On the German left, **Generaloberst Herzog Albrecht of Württemberg** (1865–1939), **Generalleutnant Kronprinz Wilhelm of Prussia** (1882–1951), **Generaloberst Kronprinz Rupprecht of Bavaria** (1869–1955) and **Generaloberst Josias von Heeringen** (1850–1926) commanded 4., 5., 6. and 7. Armeen respectively.

OPPOSING FORCES

ALLIED FORCES

Political pressure and treaty obligations undoubtedly impelled the French to launch an offensive in 1914. But their own field service regulations also played a significant role. The regulations of October 1913 were unequivocal: 'The French army, returning to its traditions, accepts no law in the conduct of operations other than the offensive… only the offensive yields positive results.' Emphasizing the importance of the will to fight, the regulations continue in similar vein: 'Battles are above all moral contests. Defeat is inevitable when the hope of victory ceases. Success comes, not to the side that has suffered the fewer losses, but to the side whose will is the steadiest and whose morale is the most highly tempered.' Defence, it was noted, 'can contain the enemy only for a limited period; it can never gain success.'

Joffre had played a major part in framing these regulations. And he was also in a position to insist that his army commanders display the 'extreme energy' required of them in the conduct of operations. But Joffre could only influence his immediate subordinates. The army had been unable to undertake any extensive peacetime manoeuvres under the new regulations. Just how far down the chain of command had the ideas they embodied been absorbed and understood?

A French headquarters in the field. A mixture of mounted and bicycle couriers await their orders: a scene familiar to every general from the days of Turenne onwards. The Marne was one of the last battles where ranges were sufficiently small to allow a general to observe his troops on the firing line.

Once battle began, accounts of French infantry attacks made without artillery support suggest that not all officers had done so. The role of the artillery was crucial to success – its mission not to prepare the attack but to support it. Artillery was to fire primarily during the attack, with the objectives of that attack forming its target. It was not to fire on enemy positions for long periods beforehand – a process described as wasteful of shells. The French field gun, the 75mm, had been introduced in 1897 and was an excellent weapon. With a maximum range of 11km (7 miles), it outranged the German 77mm, and boasted a maximum rate of fire of 28 rounds per minute. (In the field, however, this level of performance was rarely attempted; a maximum range of 5–6km (3–4 miles) was judged more realistic, while the normal firing rate was reduced to a somewhat less tiring six rounds per minute.)

However, while its field gun proved a strength, the French artillery was deficient in heavier calibres, especially howitzers. With a tactical/strategic system that placed such emphasis on mobility, some senior officers were unwilling to 'burden' the army with heavy guns. Others, including senior artillerymen, objected to increasing the number of different calibres. When a new 105mm light howitzer was proposed, they responded by suggesting a 75mm with modified ammunition – a compromise that was not a success. As a result few heavier weapons were available to the French at the outbreak of war.

But the main burden of the attack did not lie with the artillery. Once again the regulations were clear: 'To force an adversary out of his cover it is necessary to attack with the infantry.' And the 'supreme weapon' of the infantry was the bayonet. With the enemy position plastered by artillery and small-arms fire, the French infantry were to throw themselves at the foe – bayonets fixed and bugles playing – and carry the day by their superior courage and force of will.

Each infantry regiment consisted of three battalions, with a total theoretical strength of some 3,400 men, and included six machine guns. On mobilization, each infantry regiment also formed a reserve regiment of two battalions. The infantryman was armed with an 8mm 1893 Lebel rifle, with a total capacity of eight rounds, each fed singly into the magazine.

A division consisted of four infantry regiments in two brigades, an artillery regiment of nine four-gun batteries, a squadron of cavalry (usually hussars or *chasseurs à cheval*) and a company of engineers. The mobilization plan called for 46 such divisions. A further 25 reserve divisions were formed – each made up of three reserve infantry regiments. Twelve 'territorial' divisions were also created from older men for purely local defence. These units were stronger in cavalry but weaker in artillery and had no organic engineer component.

An army corps consisted of two infantry divisions. In addition, it contained two reserve infantry regiments, a cavalry regiment, an artillery regiment of 12 batteries, and four companies of engineers. This gave each corps a total strength of some 40,000 men, with 56 machine guns and 120 75mm field guns. Twelve reserve divisions were organized into 'groups' of two divisions each, but without any additional supporting elements. The French had

LEFT
French dragoons passing through Senlis. The troopers of each regiment's sabre squadrons were armed with the lance, introduced in 1883.

RIGHT
A patrol of *chasseurs d'Afrique* in Senlis, mounted on their distinctive greys. A *régiment de marche*, composed of two squadrons from the 1er Régiment and two from the 2e, served as the divisional cavalry of 45e Division d'infanterie during the battle.

21 squadrons of aircraft attached to the five armies at mobilization, with two further flights attached to 2e and 4e Divisions de cavalerie. Several aircraft were also attached to the military government of Paris.

The BEF was very small by Continental standards. At this stage it consisted of no more than five divisions and a cavalry division, plus an extra brigade of each. There was as yet no conscription, so the men were all professional soldiers. Many had seen action in the years leading up to the war, but their experience had all been gained in colonial campaigns – dismissed by many Continental observers as irrelevant to a European conflict. Yet their colonial experience was not without worth. What it had taught them was the value of marksmanship, and they made up for their smaller numbers with a high volume of accurately aimed musketry. But this was not an end in itself. Like the French (and, indeed, the Germans) the British too believed in the value of the offensive. 'The object of fire in the attack, whether of artillery, or machine guns, or infantry,' ran the pre-war training manual, 'is to bring such a superiority of fire to bear on the enemy as to make the advance to close quarters possible.'

Each infantry division consisted of three brigades – each of four battalions – a squadron of cavalry, 12 batteries of field artillery, three battalions of heavy artillery and two companies of engineers. Each infantry battalion had a theoretical strength of 1,007 men, giving a total divisional strength of just under 18,000 men. However, some battalions – those which had already fought at Mons and Le Cateau – were down to half their original strength. On mobilization each battalion was brought up to strength with reservists.

The BEF possessed little or no back-up. Many men had flocked to join up on the outbreak of war, but at this point in the conflict their training had hardly begun. The rest of the regular battalions – performing garrison duty throughout the Empire – were not immediately available. One other reserve of manpower did exist, the part-time soldiers of the Territorial Force. But the Government was most reluctant to deploy them to France. The Force was originally intended for home defence and many of its members had no direct experience of action.

The standard rifle was the Short Magazine Lee Enfield, a magazine-fed weapon with five-round clips and a maximum range of around 2,300m (2,500 yards). Each battalion also included two machine guns. The principal weapon of the field artillery was the 18-pdr field gun. This had a maximum range of 10km (six miles), while its maximum rate of fire lay between 15 and 20 rounds a minute (with a normal rate of four to eight rounds). Unlike the French, the British saw the continuing value of howitzers, even in a mobile battle. Each division included eighteen 4.5in. guns, with a range of around 6km (4 miles), and a battery of heavy 60-pdrs, with a range of about 10km (six miles). Four squadrons of the Royal Flying Corps accompanied the BEF.

GERMAN FORCES

Like its opponents, the German Army also placed great emphasis on the offensive and on the 'moral superiority' of the attacker. For the Germans too the key to victory lay in the establishment of fire superiority: 'Modern infantry combat has the character of a long, hard struggle for fire superiority. The attacker's skirmish line, carefully using the terrain and cover, can only advance slowly.'

A German infantry regiment consisted of three battalions and a machine-gun company (with six weapons), providing a total theoretical strength of some 3,200 men of all ranks. By the time of the battle most regiments had been considerably reduced in number, each now containing between 1,500 and 2,000 men. On mobilization, reservists either rejoined their parent regiment or were posted to a reserve regiment. These reserve regiments were usually organized in the same way as line regiments, although many of them lacked a machine-gun company, and some a third battalion. The German rifle was the magazine-fed Gewehr 98, which held its ammunition in five-round clips.

Like its French equivalent, the German artillery was destined to support the infantry attack as it went in, not to 'waste' ammunition by preparatory bombardments. The principal weapon of the field artillery regiments was the 77mm FK 96 n/A field gun. It had a maximum range of 7,800m (8,530 yards), and could fire about eight rounds per minute (again normal ranges were rather shorter and in the field 4,400m (4,800 yards) was regarded as long range). However, the Germans, like the British, also made use of light howitzers; they included the 105mm l.FH 98/09 in one regiment of each divisional artillery. German artillery was coordinated at the divisional level and so was more responsive to changing circumstances during an attack.

Each regular division consisted of four infantry regiments in two brigades, two regiments of artillery (12 batteries), a cavalry regiment and two companies of engineers. One division in each corps normally included an extra *Jäger* (light infantry) battalion on mobilization, but these were gradually withdrawn to serve with the cavalry. Reserve divisions were usually weaker in artillery (six batteries only) and cavalry. However, there were many variations.

An army corps consisted of two infantry divisions, plus two heavy artillery batteries (either 150mm or 210mm) and an aviation squadron. This gave each corps a paper strength of some 25,000 men (24 battalions), 48 machine guns, 108 77mm field guns, 36 105mm light howitzers and 16 150mm or 210mm heavy howitzers. The corps artillery batteries functioned simply as a reserve to bolster the divisional regiments. Reserve corps were notably weaker in supporting arms. The cavalry were formed into four cavalry corps; two of these were made up of two divisions, the other two of three. The cavalry corps all possessed attached artillery and engineers, but no infantry. During the course of the campaign, a number of *Jäger* battalions were transferred to provide them with an infantry component.

ORDERS OF BATTLE

FRENCH ORDER OF BATTLE

5e ARMÉE (GÉN. FRANCHET D'ESPEREY)
1er Corps d'armée (Gén. Deligny)
201e RI, 284e RI, 384e RM d'infanterie de réserve
1ère Division d'infanterie (Gén. Gallet)
    1ère Brigade (Col. de Fonclare)
      43e RI, 127e RI
    2e Brigade (Gén. Sauret)
      1er RI, 84e RI
2e Division d'infanterie (Gén. Deligny until 8 September, then Col. Garnier-Duplessis)
    3e Brigade (Col. Bernard)
      33e RI, 73e RI
    4e Brigade (Col. Doyen)
      8e RI, 110e RI

3e Corps d'armée (Gén. Hache)
239e RI, 274e RI
5e Division d'infanterie (Gén. Mangin)
    9e Brigade (Gén. Tassin)
      39e RI, 74e RI
    10e Brigade (Gén. Lautier)
      36e RI, 129e RI
6e Division d'infanterie (Gén. Pétain)
    11e Brigade (Col. Hériot)
      24e RI, 28e RI
    12e Brigade (Gén. Lavisse)
      5e RI, 119e RI
37e Division d'infanterie (Gén. Comby) (*until 11 September, then 6e Armée*)
    73e Brigade (Col. Degot)
      RM du 2e Zouaves, RM du 2e Tirailleurs, RM du 6e Tirailleurs, RM du 5e Tirailleurs
    74e Brigade (Col. Le Bouhélec)
      RM du 3e Zouaves, RM du 5e Tirailleurs, RM du 7e Tirailleurs

10e Corps d'armée (Gén. Desforges) (*9–11 September to 9e Armée*)
241e RI, 270e RI
19e Division d'infanterie (Gén. Bailly until the 11th, then Gén. Bonnier)
    37e Brigade (Col. Pierson)
      48e RI, 71e RI
    38e Brigade (Lt. Col. Passaga)
      41e RI, 70e RI
20e Division d'infanterie (Gén. Rogerie)
    39e Brigade (Gén. Ménissier)
      25e RI, 136e RI
    40e Brigade (Gén. de Cadoudal)
      2e RI, 47e RI
51e Division de réserve (Gén. Boutegourd)
    101e Brigade (Gén. Petit)
      233e RI, 243e RI, 327e RI
    102e Brigade (Gén. Leleu)
      208e RI, 273e RI, 310e RI

18e Corps d'armée (Gén. de Maud'huy)
218e RI, 249e RI
35e Division d'infanterie (Gén. Marjoulet)
    69e Brigade (Gén. Durand)

6e RI, 123e RI
    70e Brigade (Gén. Pierron)
      57e RI, 144e RI
36e Division d'infanterie (Gén. Jouannic)
    71e Brigade (Gén. Simon Bertin)
      34e RI, 49e RI
    72e Brigade (Gén. Trinité-Schilmans, then Col. de Sèze)
      12e RI, 18e RI
38e Division d'infanterie (Gén Schwartz)
    75e Brigade (Col. Vuillemin)
      1er RZ, 1er RT
    76e Brigade (Gén. Bertin until 6 September, then Col. Pichon)
      4e RZ, 4e RT, 8e RT

4e Groupe de division de réserve (Gén. Valabrègue)
48e BCP
53e Division d'infanterie (Gén. Perruchon until 7 September, then Gén. Journée)
    105e Brigade (Gén. Montangon)
      205e RI, 236e RI, 319e RI
    106e Brigade (Lt. Col. Masson)
      224e RI, 228e RI, 329e RI
69e Division d'infanterie (Gén. Le Gros until 12 September, then Gén. Néraud)
    137e Brigade (Gén. Rousseau)
      287e RI, 306e RI, 332e RI
    138e Brigade (Lt. Col. Piguet until 8 September, then Col. Cadoux)
      251e RI, 254e RI, 267e RI

Corps de cavalerie (Gén. Conneau)
45e RI
4e Division de cavalerie (Gén. Abonneau)
    4e Brigade légère (Gén. Requichot)
      2e RH, 4e RH
    4e Brigade de dragons (Gén. Dodelier)
      28e RD, 30e RD
    3e Brigade de cuirassiers (Gén. Sabry de Monpoly)
      3e RC, 6e RC
8e Division de cavalerie (Gén. Baratier)
    8e Brigade légère (Col. Peillard)
      12e RH, 14e RCh
    4e Brigade de dragons (Gén. Gendron until 8 September, then Col. Guéneau de Montbeillard)
      11e RD, 18e RD
10e Division de cavalerie (Gén. Grellet)
    2e Brigade légère (Gén. Contades-Gizeux)
      17e RCh, 18e RCh
    10e Brigade de dragons (Gén. Chêne)
      15e RD, 20e RD
    15e Brigade de dragons (Col. Sauzey)
      10e RD, 19e RD

6e ARMÉE (GÉN. MAUNOURY)
37e Division d'infanterie (Gén. Comby) (*from 3e Corps d'armée, 11 September*)
45e Division d'infanterie (Gén. Drude)
    89e Brigade (Col. Castaing)
      RM du 1er Zouaves, RM du 3e Zouaves
    90e Brigade (Gen. Passard)

      RM du 2e Zouaves bis, RM du 2e Tirailleurs
62e Division de réserve (Gén. Ganeval) (*8–11 September*)
    123e Brigade (Col. Peyriague)
      263e RI, 278e RI, 338e RI
    124e Brigade (Gén. Ninous)
      250e RI, 307e RI, 308e RI

Brigade Marocaine (Gén. Ditte)
    1er Régiment de chasseurs indigènes
    2e Régiment de chasseurs indigènes

4e Corps d'armée (Gén. Boëlle) (*from 7 September*)
315e RI, 317e RI
7e Division d'infanterie (Gén. de Trentinian)
    13e Brigade (Col. de Favrot)
      101e RI, 102e RI
    14e Brigade (Gén. Félineau)
      103e RI, 104e RI
8e Division d'infanterie (Gén. de Lartigue) (*under Army command, 7–9 September*)
    15e Brigade (Col. Fropo until 13 September, then Gén. Drouot)
      124e RI, 130e RI
    16e Brigade (Col. Desvaux)
      115e RI, 117e RI

7e Corps d'armée (Gén. Vautier)
352e RI, 45e BCP, 47e BCA, 55e BCP, 63e BCA, 64e BCA, 67e BCA
14e Division d'infanterie (Gén. de Villaret)
    27e Brigade (Col. Bourquin)
      44e RI, 60e RI
    28e Brigade (Gén. Faès)
      35e RI, 42e RI
63e Division de réserve (Gén. Lombard)
    125e Brigade (Gén. Dolot)
      216e RI, 238e RI, 298e RI
    126e Brigade (Gén. Guillin)
      292e RI, 305e RI, 321e RI

5e Groupe de divisions de réserve (Gén. Beaudenom de Lamaze)
55e Division de réserve (Gén. Leguay)
    109e Brigade (Gén. Arrivet)
      204e RI, 282e RI, 289e RI
    110e Brigade (Gén. Thibaudet de Mainbray)
      231e RI, 246e RI, 276e RI
56e Division de réserve (Gén. de Dartein)
    111e Brigade (Lt. Col. Bonne)
      294e RI, 354e RI, 355e RI
    112e Brigade (Gén. Cornille)
      350e RI, 361e RI, 65e BCP, 66e BCP, 69e BCP

6e Groupe de divisions de réserve (Gén. Eberner) (*from 11 September*)
61e Division de réserve (Gén. Déprez)
    121e Brigade (Gén. Delarue)
      264e RI, 265e RI, 316e RI
    122e Brigade (Lt. Col. Tesson)
      219e RI, 262e RI, 318e RI
62e Division de réserve (Gén. Ganeval)
    123e Brigade (Col. Peyriague)

263e RI, 278e RI, 338e RI
124e Brigade (Gén. Ninous)
250e RI, 307e RI, 308e RI
Brigade de spahis (Col. Martin du Bouillon)
(from 10 September)
1er RMSA
2e RMSA

Corps de cavalerie (Gén. Sordet until 8 September, then Gén. Bridoux)
1ère Division de cavalerie (Gén. Buisson)
5e Brigade de dragons (Gén. Silvestre)
6e RD, 23e RD
11e Brigade de dragons (Gén. Corvisart)
27e RD, 32e RD
2e Brigade de cuirassiers (Gén. Louvat)
1er RC, 2e RC
3e Division de cavalerie (Gén. de Lastours)
3e Brigade légère (Gén. de la Villestreux)
3e RH, 8e RH
13e Brigade de dragons (Gén. Léorat)
5e RD, 21e RD
4e Brigade de cuirassiers (Gén. Gouzil)
4e RC, 9e RC
5e Division de cavalerie (Gén. Bridoux until 10 September, then Gén. Lallemand du Marais)
5e Brigade légère (Gén. de Cornulier-Lucinière)
5e RCh, 15e RCh
3e Brigade de dragons (Gén. Lallemand du Marais)
13e RD, 22e RD
7e Brigade de dragons (Gén. Emé de Marcieux)
9e RD, 29e RD

9e ARMÉE (DÉTACHEMENT D'ARMÉE FOCH UNTIL 6 SEPTEMBER) (GÉN. FOCH)
9e Division de cavalerie (Gén. de l'Espée) *(until 10 September)*
9e Brigade de dragons (Gén. Sailly)
1er RD, 3e RD
16e Brigade de dragons (Gén. Gombaud)
24e RD, 25e RD
4e Brigade de cuirassiers (Col. Cugnac)
5e RC, 8e RC
42e Division d'infanterie (Gén. Grossetti)
83e Brigade (Gén. Krien)
94e RI, 8e BCP, 16e BCP, 19e BCP
84e Brigade (Col. Trouchard)
151e RI, 162e RI

9e Corps d'armée (Gén. Dubois)
268e RI, 290e RI
17e Division d'infanterie (Gén. Moussy)
33e Brigade (Col. Simon until 13 September, then Gén. Moussy)
68e RI, 90e RI
36e Brigade (Col. Eon)
77e RI, 135e RI
Division Marocaine (Gén. Humbert)
1ère Brigade (Gén. Blondlat)
RM colonial, RM de zouaves
2e Brigade (Lt. Col. Cros)
1er RM de tirailleurs du Maroc occidental, 2e RM de tirailleurs du Maroc oriental
52e Division de réserve (Gén. Battesti)
103e Brigade (Col. Doursout, then Lt. Col. Lévy, then from 9 September Lt. Col. Guyot de Salins)
291e RI, 347e RI, 348e RI
104e Brigade (Lt. Col. Claudon)
245e RI, 320e RI, 49e BCP, 58e BCP
18e Division d'infanterie (Gén. Lefèvre)
34e Brigade (Gén. Guignabaudet, then from 14 September Col. Simon)
114e RI, 125e RI
35e Brigade (Col. Janin)
32e RI, 66e RI

10e Corps d'armée (from 5e Armée, 9–11 September)

11e Corps d'armée (Gén. Eydoux) (from 5e Armée, 8 September)
293e RI, 337e RI
21e Division d'infanterie (Gén. Radiguet)
41e Brigade (Col. de Teyssière)
64e RI, 65e RI
42e Brigade (Col. Lamey until 8 September, then Col. Bouyssou)
93e RI, 137e RI
22e Division d'infanterie (Gén. Pambet)
43e Brigade (Gén. Costebonel)

62e RI, 116e RI
44e Brigade (Gén. Chaplain)
19e RI, 118e RI
60e Division de réserve (Gén. Joppé)
119e Brigade (Gén. Reveilhac)
247e RI, 248e RI, 271e RI
120e Brigade (Gén. Margueron)
202e RI, 225e RI, 336e RI

21e Corps d'armée (Gén. Maistre)
13e Division d'infanterie (Gén. Baquet)
25e Brigade (Col. Griache)
17e RI, 17e BCP, 20e BCP, 21e BCP
26e Brigade (Lt. Col. Schmidt)
21e RI, 109e RI
43e Division d'infanterie (Gén. Lanquetot)
85e Brigade (Col. Menvielle)
149e RI, 158e RI
86e Brigade (Col. Olleris)
1er BCP, 3e BCP, 20e BCP, 31e BCP

Key to abbreviations:

BCA	*Bataillon de chasseurs alpins*
BCP	*Bataillon de chasseurs à pied*
RC	*Régiment de cuirassiers*
RCA	*Régiment de chasseurs d'Afrique*
RCh	*Régiment de chasseurs à cheval*
RD	*Régiment de dragons*
RH	*Régiment de hussards*
RI	*Régiment d'infanterie*
RM	*Régiment de marche*
RMSA	*Régiment de marche de spahis algériens*
RT	*Régiment de tirailleurs*
RZ	*Régiment de zouaves*

BRITISH ORDER OF BATTLE

BRITISH EXPEDITIONARY FORCE (FIELD MARSHAL SIR JOHN FRENCH)
Cavalry Division (Maj. Gen. Allenby)
1st Cavalry Brigade
2nd Dragoon Guards
5th Dragoon Guards
11th Hussars
2nd Cavalry Brigade
4th Dragoon Guards
9th Lancers
18th Hussars
3rd Cavalry Brigade
4th Hussars
5th Lancers
16th Lancers
4th Cavalry Brigade
Household Cavalry Regiment
6th Dragoon Guards
3rd Hussars

5th Cavalry Brigade/Gough's Command (Brig. Gen. Gough)
2nd Dragoons
12th Lancers
20th Hussars.

I Corps (Lt. Gen. Sir Douglas Haig)
1st Division (Maj. Gen. Lomax)
1st (Guards) Brigade
1st Coldstream Guards
1st Scots Guards
1st Black Watch
1st Cameron Highlanders
2nd Infantry Brigade
2nd Royal Sussex Regiment
1st Loyal North Lancashire Regiment
1st Northamptonshire Regiment
2nd King's Royal Rifle Corps
3rd Infantry Brigade
1st Queen's Regiment
1st South Wales Borderers
1st Gloucestershire Regiment
2nd Welch Regiment
2nd Division (Maj. Gen. Monro)
4th (Guards) Brigade
2nd Grenadier Guards
2nd Coldstream Guards
3rd Coldstream Guards
1st Irish Guards
5th Infantry Brigade
2nd Worcester Regiment
2nd Ox. & Bucks. Light Infantry

2nd Highland Light Infantry
2nd Connaught Rangers
6th Infantry Brigade
1st King's Regiment
2nd South Staffordshire Regiment
1st Royal Berkshire Regiment
1st King's Royal Rifle Corps

II Corps (Gen. Sir Horace Smith-Dorrien)
3rd Division (Maj. Gen. Hamilton)
7th Infantry Brigade
3rd Worcester Regiment
2nd South Lancashire Regiment
1st Wiltshire Regiment
2nd Royal Irish Rifles
8th Infantry Brigade
2nd Royal Scots Regiment
2nd Royal Irish Regiment
4th Middlesex Regiment
1st Gordon Highlanders
9th Infantry Brigade
1st Northumberland Fusiliers
4th Royal Fusiliers
1st Lincolnshire Regiment
1st Royal Scots Fusiliers
5th Division (Maj. Gen. Fergusson)
13th Infantry Brigade
2nd King's Own Scottish Borderers
2nd Duke of Wellington's Regiment
1st Royal West Kent Regiment
2nd King's Own Yorkshire Light Infantry
14th Infantry Brigade
2nd Suffolk Regiment
1st East Surrey Regiment
1st Duke of Cornwall's Light Infantry
2nd Manchester Regiment
15th Infantry Brigade
1st Norfolk Regiment
1st Bedfordshire Regiment
1st Cheshire Regiment
1st Dorsetshire Regiment

III Corps (Lt. Gen. Pulteney)
4th Division (Maj. Gen. Snow until the 9th, then Brigadier H. Wilson)
10th Infantry Brigade
1st Royal Warwickshire Regiment
2nd Seaforth Highlanders
1st Royal Irish Fusiliers
2nd Royal Dublin Fusiliers
11th Infantry Brigade
1st Somerset Light Infantry
1st East Lancashire Regiment
1st Hampshire Regiment
1st Rifle Brigade
12th Infantry Brigade
1st King's Own Regiment
2nd Lancashire Fusiliers
2nd Royal Inniskilling Fusiliers
2nd Essex Regiment

19th Brigade (Maj. Gen. Drummond)
2nd Royal Welsh Fusiliers
1st Cameronians
1st Middlesex Regiment
2nd Argyll and Sutherland Highlanders

GERMAN ORDER OF BATTLE

1. ARMEE (GEN.OBST. VON KLUCK)
II Armeekorps (Gen. der Inf. von Linsingen)
3. Infanterie-Division (Gen.Lt. von Trossel)
5. Infanterie-Brigade (Gen.Maj. Freiherr Treusch von Buttlar-Brandenfels)
Gren.R. 2, Gren.R. 9
6. Infanterie-Brigade (Obst. Gräser)
Füs.R. 34, IR 42
4. Infanterie-Division (Gen.Lt. von Pannewitz)
7. Infanterie-Brigade (Gen.Maj. von Runckel)
IR 14, IR 149
8. Infanterie-Brigade (Obst. Jennrich)
IR 49, IR 140

III Armeekorps (Gen. der Inf. von Lochow)
5. Infanterie-Division (Gen.Lt. Wichura)
9. Infanterie-Brigade (Gen.Maj. von Doemming)
Gren.R. 8, IR 48
10. Infanterie-Brigade (Gen.Maj. Sontag)

Gren.R. 12, IR 52
6. Infanterie-Division (Gen.Maj. Herhudt von Rohden)
  11. Infanterie-Brigade (Gen.Maj. von Wachter)
    Füs.R. 35, IR 20
  12. Infanterie-Brigade (Gen.Maj. von Gabain)
    IR 24, IR 64

IV Armeekorps (Gen. der Inf. Sixt von Armin)
7. Infanterie-Division (Gen.Lt. Riedel)
  13. Infanterie-Brigade (Gen.Maj. von Schüßler)
    IR 26, IR 66
  14. Infanterie-Brigade (Gen.Maj. von Oven)
    IR 27, IR 165
8. Infanterie-Division (Gen.Lt. Hildebrandt)
  15. Infanterie-Brigade (Gen.Maj. Reichenau)
    Füs.R. 36, IR 93
  16. Infanterie-Brigade (Gen.Maj. von Jaroßky)
    IR 72, IR 153

IX Armeekorps (Gen. der Inf. von Quast)
17. Infanterie-Division (Gen.Lt. von Bauer)
  33. Infanterie-Brigade (Gen.Maj. von Kraewel)
    IR 75, IR 76
  34. Infanterie-Brigade (Gen.Maj. von Lewinski)
    Gren.R. 89, Füs.R. 90
18. Infanterie-Division (Gen.Lt. von Kluge)
  35. Infanterie-Brigade (Obst. von Obernitz)
    IR 84, Füs.R. 86
  36. Infanterie-Brigade (Gen.Maj. Freiherr von Troschke)
    IR 31, IR 85

IV Reservekorps (Gen. der Art. von Gronau)
7. Reserve-Division (Gen.Lt. Graf von Schwerin)
  13. Reserve-Infanterie-Brigade (Gen.Maj. von Dressler und Scharfenstein)
    RIR 27, RIR 36
  14. Reserve-Infanterie-Brigade (Gen.Maj. von Wienstowski)
    RIR 66, RIR 72, R.Jäg.Batl.4
22. Reserve-Division (Gen.Lt. Riemann)
  43. Reserve-Infanterie-Brigade (Gen.Maj. von Lepel)
    RIR 71, RIR 94, R.Jäg.Batl. 11
  44. Reserve-Infanterie-Brigade (Gen.Maj. von Mühlenfels)
    RIR 32, RIR 82

Höherer Kavallerie-Kommandeur 2 (Gen.der Kav. von der Marwitz)
Jäg.Batl. 3, Jäg.Batl. 4, Jäg.Batl. 7, Jäg.Batl. 9
2. Kavallerie-Division (Gen.Maj. Freiherr von Krane):
    Drag.R. 2, Ul.R. 3
    Kur.R. 7, Hus.R.12
    Lb.Hus.R.1, Lb.Hus.R.2
4. Kavallerie-Division (Gen.Lt. von Garnier)
  3. Kavallerie-Brigade (Gen.Maj. Graf von Schimmelmann)
    Kür.R. 2, Ul.R. 9
  17. Kavallerie-Brigade (Obst. Graf von der Goltz)
    Drag.R. 17, Drag.R. 18
  18. Kavallerie-Brigade (Obst. von Printz)
    Hus.R. 15, Hus.R. 16
9. Kavallerie-Division (Gen.Maj. Graf Eberhard von Schmettow)
  13. Kavallerie-Brigade (Obst. Selfert)
    Kür.R. 4, Hus.R. 8
  14. Kavallerie-Brigade (Obst. von Heuduck)
    Hus.R. 11, Ul.R. 5
  19. Kavallerie-Brigade (Obstlt. von Preinitzer)
    Drag.R. 19, Ul.R. 13

N.B. III Reservekorps, and 11. and 27. gem. Ldw.Br., also part of this Army, were on lines of communications duties, and were not engaged in the battle; IX Reservekorps was still in Germany.

2. ARMEE (GEN.OBST. VON BÜLOW)
Gardekorps (Gen. der Inf. Freiherr von Plettenberg)
1. Garde-Infanterie-Division (Gen.Lt. von Hutier)
  1. Garde-Infanterie-Brigade (Gen.Maj. von Kleist)
    1. G.R.z.Fß., 3. G.R.z.Fß.
  2. Garde-Infanterie-Brigade (Gen.Maj. Schach von Wittenau until 6 September, then Oberst von dem Busch)
    2. G.R.z.Fß., 4. G.R.z.Fß.
2. Garde-Infanterie-Division (Gen.Lt. von Winckler)
  3. Garde-Infanterie-Brigade (Gen.Maj. von Petersdorff)
    G.Gren.R. 1, G.Gren.R. 3
  4. Garde-Infanterie-Brigade (Gen.Maj. von Gontard)
    G.Gren.R. 2, G.Gren.R. 4

VII Armeekorps (Gen. der Kav. von Einem)
13. Infanterie-Division (Gen.Lt. von dem Borne)
  25. Infanterie-Brigade (Gen.Maj. von Unruh)
    IR 13, IR 158
  26. Infanterie-Brigade
    IR 15, IR 55 (at Maubeuge)
14. Infanterie-Division (Gen.Lt. Fleck)
  27. Infanterie-Brigade (Obst. von Massow)
    IR 16, IR 53
  79. Infanterie-Brigade (Gen.Maj. Schwarte)
    IR 56, IR 57

X Armeekorps (Gen. der Inf. von Emmich)
19. Infanterie-Division (Gen.Lt. Hoffman)
  37. Infanterie-Brigade (Obst. Freiherr von Gregory)
    IR 78, IR 91
  38. Infanterie-Brigade (Obst. von Dertzen)
    Füs.R. 73, IR 74
20. Infanterie-Division (Gen.Lt. Schmundt)
  39. Infanterie-Brigade (Gen.Maj. von L'Estocq)
    IR 79, IR 164
  40. Infanterie-Brigade (Obst. Graf zu Rantzau)
    IR 77, IR 92

X Reservekorps (Gen. der Inf. von Eben)
2. Garde-Reserve-Division (Gen. der Inf. Freiherr von Süßkind)
  26. Reserve-Infanterie-Brigade (Obst. Cotta until 6 September, then Maj. von Wißmann on the 6th only, then Maj. Springefeld)
    RIR 15, RIR 55
  38. Reserve-Infanterie-Brigade (Obstlt. Wünsche)
    RIR 77, RIR 91, R.Jäg.Batl.10
19. Reserve-Division (Gen.Lt. von Bahrfeldt)
  37. Reserve-Infanterie-Brigade (Obst. von Winterfeldt)
    RIR 73, RIR 78
  39. Reserve-Infanterie-Brigade (Gen.Maj. von Wright)
    RIR 74, RIR 92, III./RIR 79

Höherer Kavallerie-Kommandeur 1 (Gen.Lt. Freiherr von Richthofen)
Garde-Kavallerie-Division (Gen.Lt. von Storch)
  1. Garde-Kavallerie-Brigade (Obst. von Barensprung)
    Garde du Corps, G.Kür.R.
  2. Garde-Kavallerie-Brigade (Gen.Maj. Graf von Rothkirch und Trach)
    G.Ul.R. 1, G.Ul.R. 3
  3. Garde-Kavallerie-Brigade (Obst. Freiherr von Senden)
    G.Drag.R. 1, G.Drag.R. 2, G.Jäg.Batl.

5. Kavallerie-Division (Gen.Maj. von Ilsemann)
  9. Kavallerie-Brigade (Gen.Maj. Rusche)
    Drag.R. 4, Ul.R. 6
  11. Kavallerie-Brigade (Obst. von Wentzky und Petersheyde)
    Kür.R. 1, Drag.R. 8
  12. Kavallerie-Brigade (Gen.Maj. Graf von Pfeil und Klein-Ellguth)
    Hus.R. 4, Hus.R. 6, G.Schü.Batl.

N.B. VII Reservekorps, and 25. and 29. gem.Ldw.Br., also part of this Army, were on lines of communications duties, and were not engaged in the battle.

3. ARMEE (GEN.OBST. FREIHERR VON HAUSEN)
XII Armeekorps (Gen. der Inf. d'Elsa)
23. Infanterie-Division (Gen.Lt. Freiherr von Lindenau)
  45. Infanterie-Brigade (Gen.Maj. Lucius)
    Lb.Gren.R. 100, Gren.R. 101
  46. Infanterie-Brigade (Gen.Maj. von Watzdorff)
    Schü.-(Füs.-)R. 108, IR 182
32. Infanterie-Division (Gen.Lt. Edler von der Planitz)
  63. Infanterie-Brigade (Gen.Maj. von Gersdorff)
    IR 102, IR 103, Jäg.Batl. 12
  64. Infanterie-Brigade (Gen.Maj. Morgenstern-Döring)
    IR 177, IR 178

XII Reservekorps (Gen. der Art. von Kirchbach)
47.gem. Ldw.Br.,
    Ldw.IR 104, Ldw.IR 106
23. Reserve-Division (Gen.Lt. von Larisch)
  45. Reserve-Infanterie-Brigade (Gen.Lt. von Suckow)
    R.Gren.R. 100, RIR 101, R.Jäg.Batl. 12
  46. Reserve-Infanterie-Brigade (Gen.Lt. Hempel)
    RIR 102, RIR 103
24. Reserve-Division (Gen.Lt. von Ehrenthal) (*at Givet; did not rejoin until 7 September*)
  47. Reserve-Infanterie-Brigade (Gen.Lt. Ullrich)
    RIR 104, RIR 106, R.Jäg.Batl. 13
  48. Reserve-Infanterie-Brigade (Gen.Lt. Wilhelm)
    RIR 107, RIR 133

N.B.: XIX Armeekorps, although part of this army, was facing French 4e Armée.

Key to abbreviations:

Batl.	*Bataillon*
Br.	*Brigade*
Drag.	*Dragoner*
Esk.	*Eskadron*
Füs.	*Füsilier*
G.	*Garde*
Gem.	*Gemischte*
Gren.	*Grenadier*
Hus.	*Husaren*
IR	*Infanterie-Regiment*
Jäg.Batl.	*Jäger Bataillon*
Komp.	*Kompagnie*
Kür.	*Kürassier*
Lb.	*Leib*
Ldst.	*Landsturm*
Ldw.	*Landwehr*
Lb.Gren.	*Leib Grenadier*
R	*Reserve*
RIR	*Reserve- Infanterie-Regiment*
Sächs.	*Sächsische*
Schü.	*Schützen*
Ul.	*Uhlan*

OPPOSING PLANS

The failure of the French offensives in the battles of the Frontiers forced Joffre to reconsider his options. Watching the German advance develop, Joffre realized he had an opportunity to strike at the enemy right, in the relatively open country of northern France, rather than the wooded hills and valleys of the east. From 25 August he began to assemble his forces on the open right flank of the German army – initially around Amiens. These men would go on to become the nucleus of 6e Armée. Most of them had come from the French right wing in Alsace. Here the enemy could do nothing to penetrate the line of fortifications along the Moselle, and attacks by 6. Armee (Kronprinz Rupprecht) and more particularly by 7. Armee (Heeringen), around Dieuze and Lunéville, had been driven back by well-sited artillery.

Moltke was well aware that Joffre was moving men from right to left, and a new urgency overtook him as he tried to find a way of striking the decisive blow before the effect of the transfer could be felt. On 27 August – encouraged by what he saw as a defeated enemy in full retreat – he decided to attack on all fronts. 1. Armee (Kluck) was to skirt the French capital to the west, while 2. Armee (Bülow) aimed directly at the city itself. 3. Armee (Hausen), 4. Armee (Herzog von Württemberg) and 5. Armee (Kronprinz Wilhelm) were to head towards the line Château-Thierry–Epernay–Vitry-le-François. Meanwhile 6. and 7. Armeen were to attack along the Moselle and break through between Toul and Epinal.

'En route to Berlin'. These men from the administrative sections of 14e Corps d'armée, based in Lyon, would never get anywhere near the German capital.

The 18-pdr guns of 49th Battery, Royal Field Artillery, on the move through a French town.

But gaps had begun to appear in the German line. The advance was starting to take its toll. Back in Belgium two reserve corps had been left behind to mask Antwerp and garrison Brussels, while the equivalent of another corps was investing the towns of Givet, on the Meuse, and Maubeuge. Then on 25 August came alarming news of Russian advances in the east. Confident that he had achieved a decisive victory in the battles of the Frontiers, and under considerable political pressure to bolster German forces in that theatre, Moltke detached a corps each from 2. and 3. Armeen and sent them to eastern Prussia.

The remaining troops had to cover these gaps, as well perform their original duties. Hausen's men were marching an average of 23km (14 miles) a day; Kluck's, 30km (19 miles). But the Belgians had destroyed much of the railway infrastructure before the enemy advance, and the German supply echelons could not keep up. Horses ate grain straight from the fields; men marched whole days on nothing but raw carrots and cabbages.

While his right wing continued on its south-west axis, the logic of Moltke's orders was to pull the main thrust of his attack south and south-east. The attacks along the Moselle – and the tough fighting encountered there – pulled 4. and 5. Armeen further in that direction to relieve the pressure on 6. and 7. Armeen by attacking the rear of France's eastern fortifications. Hausen – in the centre – was now finding it increasingly difficult to keep contact with Bülow to his right. Instead of continuing south-westwards in tandem with 1. and 2. Armeen, he too was forced to turn south to support 4. Armee on his left.

On 29 August Joffre ordered limited counterattacks by his 3e, 4e and 5e Armées in an attempt to buy more time for his regrouping manoeuvres. The 5e Armée (Lanrezac) attacked Bülow's right flank and at Guise pushed it back some 5km (3 miles). Losses on both sides were high. More crucially, Bülow had to order a 36-hour pause in the advance for his men to recover, and requested the support of Kluck.

Overview of the battle of the Marne, 5–9 September 1914

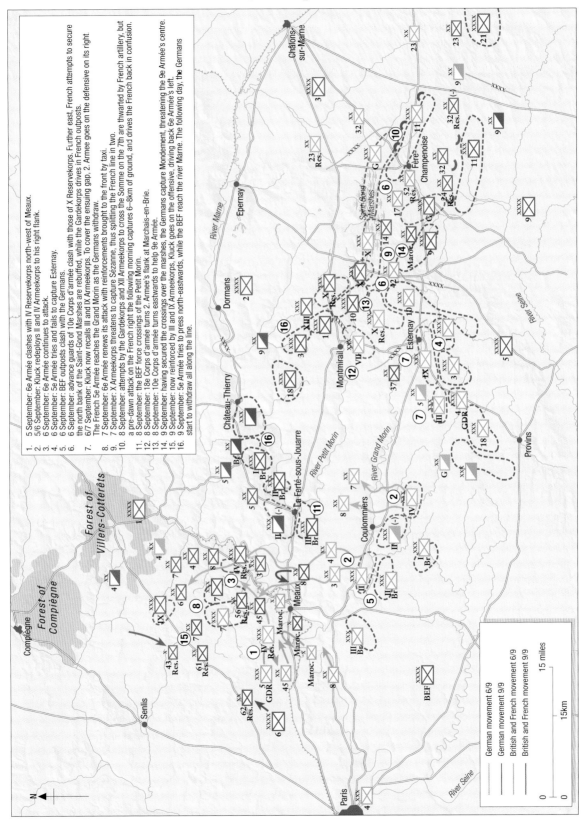

1. 5 September: 6e Armée clashes with IV Reservekorps north-west of Meaux.
2. 5/6 September: Kluck redeploys II and IV Armeekorps to his right flank.
3. 6 September: 6e Armée continues to attack.
4. 6 September: 5e Armée tries and fails to capture Esternay.
5. 6 September: BEF outposts clash with the Germans.
6. 6 September: advance guards of 10e Corps d'armée clash with those of X Reservekorps. Further east, French attempts to secure the north bank of the Saint-Gond Marshes are rebuffed, while the Gardekorps drives in French outposts.
7. 6/7 September: Kluck now recalls III and IX Armeekorps. To cover the ensuing gap, 2. Armee goes on the defensive on its right. The French 5e Armée reaches the Grand Morin as the Germans withdraw.
8. 7 September: 6e Armée renews its attack with reinforcements brought to the front by taxi.
9. 7 September: X Armeekorps threatens to capture Sézanne, thus splitting the French line in two.
10. 8 September: attempts by the Gardekorps and XII Armeekorps to cross the Somme on the 7th are thwarted by French artillery, but a pre-dawn attack on the French right the following morning captures 6–8km of ground, and drives the French back in confusion.
11. 8 September: the BEF force crossings of the Petit Morin.
12. 8 September: 18e Corps d'armée turns 2. Armee's flank at Marchais-en-Brie.
13. 8 September: 10e Corps d'armée turns eastwards to help 9e Armée.
14. 9 September: having secured the crossings over the marshes, the Germans capture Mondement, threatening the 9e Armée's centre.
15. 9 September: now reinforced by III and IX Armeekorps, Kluck goes on the offensive, driving back 6e Armée's left.
16. 9 September: 5e Armée tries to press north-eastwards, while the BEF reach the river Marne. The following day, the Germans start to withdraw all along the line.

German movement 6/9
German movement 9/9
British and French movement 6/9
British and French movement 9/9

0   15 miles
0   15km

25

A rather ramshackle collection of wagons, supplying a regiment of *zouaves*. Each infantry battalion included a *train de combat* – 54 wagons strong – containing reserves of food and ammunition, the company cookers and the medical officer's wagon. The regimental HQ also had a second echelon containing a further 20 wagons, carrying extra reserves of food.

Meanwhile, Moltke was increasingly concerned about the gaps now appearing between the armies of his centre and right. On 29 August he ordered changes in their axes of advance to bring them closer together. 2., 3. and 5. Armeen were to advance southwards, while 1. Armee turned in a south-easterly direction. Had Kluck continued on his previous line of march, he would undoubtedly have disrupted the build-up of 6e Armée (Maunoury) – and possibly gone on to envelop the BEF. As it was, he now threatened the rear of 5e Armée.

The German advance had been momentarily checked, but the Allied armies continued to withdraw out of harm's way. The attitude of the British remained unclear. Armed with permission from London to pulll back towards the coast in the event of a German victory – and unduly pessimistic about the condition of his men – Sir John French refused to support 5e Armée in its attacks. Indeed, he threatened to withdraw completely – if necessary as far as the new BEF base depot at Saint-Nazaire on the Atlantic coast.

Such a move would force the new 6e Armée to replace the BEF in the Allied line, and the chance of enveloping the German right would be lost for ever. Only the combined efforts of Lord Kitchener, then secretary of war, and Joffre himself persuaded Sir John to cooperate. However, the retreat of the BEF did have one unexpected benefit. It removed the British completely from sight of the German advanced elements.

Joffre had originally intended to hold a line along the rivers Somme and Oise. But the pressure exerted by the Germans, and the precipitate withdrawal of the BEF, had now made this impossible. Joffre ordered a further retreat – this time as far as the southern bank of the Seine – but still hoped his forces might be able to halt before reaching that line, possibly on the river Marne.

On 31 August the French launched further counterattacks west of Verdun. Designed to realign the front line and allow the newly formed 9e Armée (Foch) to enter the battle, these were of only limited duration. But when they ceased Moltke assumed that a general counterattack had been defeated. And on 2 September he ordered further changes in the direction of the German advance to take advantage of what he perceived as French disarray. Taking up a position on Bülow's right flank, and somewhat to his rear, 1. Armee was to turn to face west in order to screen Paris. Far from leading the offensive, Kluck's role was now to guard the German right wing. Moltke's stated intention was to drive the French south-eastwards – a sudden shift in strategy from envelopment to breakthrough.

But 1. Armee was by now some kilometres in advance of Bülow. Kluck was convinced that the BEF was permanently out of action and that the French forces on his flank were scattered units incapable of a concerted attack. If he stopped now he might lose the chance to envelop 5e Armée. Ignoring Moltke's latest orders as irrelevant to the situation on the ground, he decided to continue with his rapid advance.

Back in Luxembourg, Moltke was having second thoughts. What if the French forces now gathered around Paris attacked the flank of 1. Armee as it marched? On 4 September he issued new orders. While 6. and 7. Armeen continued their attacks in Alsace, in an attempt to take advantage of French troop withdrawals, 4. and 5. Armeen were to attack south-eastwards. The aim was to trap the French around Verdun and Nancy. The 1. Armee – now joined by 2. Armee – would resume its role as flank guard. And, in the centre, 3. Armee would hold its position. With these new orders, the emphasis of the German invasion had definitively shifted. It was now seeking a decision in just that fortified area of eastern France that Schlieffen's original plan had tried so hard to avoid.

Kluck did not receive these new orders until 0700hrs on 5 September – after the day's march had begun – and was still in no mood to be relegated to the subordinate position intended for him. Only a visit that afternoon from Oberstleutnant Richard Hentsch, the OHL (Oberste Heeresleitung – German Supreme Headquarters) head of intelligence persuaded him to accept his new role. But Kluck remained convinced that the BEF and the French in front of him had been defeated and thus posed no threat: 'The British have been beaten repeatedly and will scarcely be induced to come forward quickly and form a powerful offensive.'

The flank guard 1. Armee, IV Reservekorps, had no aviation component and relied on its cavalry to warn of any approaching attack. But there seemed to be nothing to worry about. All was quiet in that sector.

THE FIRST BATTLE OF THE MARNE

Général Maunoury, commander of 6e Armée. After the battle, he said to his men, 'It is with deep emotion that I thank you for giving me what all my efforts, all my energy have been directed towards for 43 years: revenge for 1870.'

THE BATTLE OF THE OURCQ, 5–9 SEPTEMBER

The French were soon aware that the Germans had changed direction. German signal discipline was poor, and some messages, sent in the clear, were duly intercepted. Aerial observation by aircraft operating out of Paris further confirmed this intelligence. Général Gallieni, newly appointed military governor of Paris, immediately proposed that 6e Armée should attack on the open German right flank. But Joffre was less certain. He was reluctant to move prematurely, wanting to be sure of the position in the centre of his line before committing all his forces to battle.

Gallieni was primarily concerned for the safety of the capital city. For Joffre, however, Paris was simply 'a geographical expression'. Its safety would best be assured by victory in the field. But this would require a little more time. Joffre's own aerial reconnaissance reported that Kluck's men were continuing to move south-east. Extra forces in the form of 6e and 9e Armées were now close to readiness. The armies of the French centre and right had all stabilized their fronts. And the BEF had finally agreed to play its part. Taking everything into account, Joffre predicted that his battle would begin on 7 September.

Joffre issued his orders accordingly. 6e Armée was to advance eastwards across the river Ourcq between Lizy-sur-Ourcq and May-en-Multien and then continue forwards in the direction of Château-Thierry. The BEF, by now some 8km (5 miles) south of the Grand Morin, was to advance eastwards towards Montmirail. 5e Armée (Franchet d'Esperey) was to wait until the BEF had attracted German attention and then drive northwards, its right flank covered by the 9e (Foch).

Joffre's order of the day was unequivocal: 'Now, as the battle is joined on which the safety of the country depends, everyone must be reminded that this is no longer the time for looking back. Every effort must be made to attack and throw back the enemy. A unit which finds it impossible to advance must, regardless of cost, hold its ground and be killed on the spot rather than fall back. In the present circumstances no failure will be tolerated.'

Although 6e Armée constituted the main French strike force, it was hardly fit for action. Many formations had already seen combat. 7e Corps d'armée (Vautier) had lost some 3,000 men in Alsace. 5e Groupe de division de réserve (Lamaze) – now strengthened by the addition of 45e Division d'infanterie from Algeria and a brigade of untried infantry supplied by the Sultan of Morocco – had fought on the Meuse. The men of 6e Groupe de divisions de

The battle of the Ourcq, 5–9 September 1914

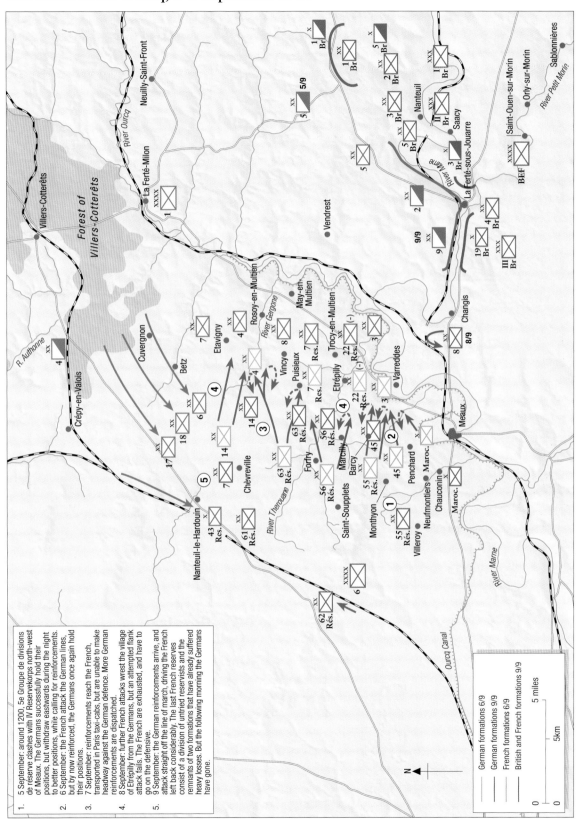

1. 5 September: around 1200, 5e Groupe de divisions de reserve clashes with IV Reservekorps north-west of Meaux. The Germans successfully hold their positions, but withdraw eastwards during the night to better positions, while calling for reinforcements.

2. 6 September: the French attack the German lines, but by now reinforced, the Germans once again hold their positions.

3. 7 September: reinforcements reach the French, transported in Paris taxi-cabs, but are unable to make headway against the German defence. More German reinforcements are dispatched.

4. 8 September: further French attacks wrest the village of Etrépilly from the Germans, but an attempted flank attack fails. The French are exhausted, and have to go on the defensive.

5. 9 September: the German reinforcements arrive, and attack straight off the line of march, driving the French left back considerably. The last French reserves consist of a division of untried reservists and the remnants of two formations that have already suffered heavy losses. But the following morning the Germans have gone.

Key:
— German formations 6/9
— German formations 9/9
— French formations 6/9
— British and French formations 9/9

N

0 ———— 5 miles
0 ———— 5km

29

LEFT
Looking north-east towards Monthyon. From the farm on the right of the village the first shots of the battle were fired.

RIGHT
On 5 September 55e Division d'infanterie advanced from left to right across this ground. The line of trees in the distance marks the end of the road from Villeroy; the clump of trees immediately to the right marks the grave of the men of 55e and 56e Divisions d'infanterie. The Germans, men of IR 66, occupied the shallow slope on the right.

BOTTOM
Moroccan *chasseurs*. These regiments were not part of the French Army. They were raised in Morocco, with a mixture of French and Moroccan officers and NCOs, to assist in the pacification of that country. As they marched, they chanted, 'We come from Moulay Idriss [the Sultan]/May God forgive our sins'.

réserve (Eberner) had clashed with 1. Armee in skirmishes around Cambrai: Gallieni thought them exhausted and expected little of them. Sordet's Corps de cavalerie provided the cavalry component. But its horses were already worn out by incessant marching and poor fodder. Also on its way to provide extra reinforcements was 4e Corps d'armée (Boëlle). Like the 7e, it had already endured heavy losses. Beset by transport difficulties, it would arrive in penny packets from 5 to 7 September.

To get into position 6e Armée had to move immediately. From his headquarters at Le Raincy, on the outskirts of Paris, Maunoury sent out his orders: the advance would begin early in the morning of 5 September. Issued in a hurry, and at the last minute, these orders had nothing to say about the likely strength of the opposing forces. There had been no time for such niceties as strategic reconnaissance, even had the cavalry been ready and willing to undertake it. Issued at midnight, Maunoury's orders did not reach the front-line regiments, some 20km (16 miles) away, until 0600hrs – a mere hour before the advance was to begin. The French believed the main body of Kluck's 1. Armee to be crossing the Marne, advancing south-eastwards. So they expected to face little more than a few scattered flank guards or rear echelons.

5 September

In fact, the Germans were present in much greater strength than anticipated. The main body of 1. Armee was by now well south of the Marne. Indeed, by the morning of 5 September, its leading elements were advancing south of the Grand Morin. However, some formations still remained north of the Marne. Along with 4. Kavallerie-Division, the men of Gronau's IV Reservekorps (7. and 22. Reserve-Divisionen) were some 25km (16 miles) further north than expected and had passed the night around Nanteuil-le-Haudouin. Moving south they paused for a meal around 1100hrs near the villages of Barcy and Chambry. Suddenly German cavalry – more alert than their French counterparts – noticed enemy activity in the villages just over a kilometre away to the west. Gronau now faced a dilemma. His men had not yet seen action and were tired after days of marching under a hot sun. As reserve divisions, his forces were also weaker in artillery than their regular counterparts. And dropping off troops for lines of communications duties had reduced them still further. Only 16 of Gronau's 25 battalions had all four companies present. Many of the cavalry horses had been requisitioned from farms and were unsuitable for their role. And the corps signals detachment was short of men and spare parts. Should he risk an attack against an enemy of unknown strength?

The French advanced guards had also halted for midday refreshments. The sun was hot and they had decided to pause at Plessis-l'Evêque and Iverny before advancing over the line of low hills to their front.

Gronau made his decision: 'There is no help for it, we must attack.' At 1230hrs three batteries of Reserve-Feldartillerie-Regiment 7 opened fire on the villages held by the French. The battle of the Marne had begun.

Caught by surprise, the French still managed to respond immediately. One battery of 75s began counter-battery fire, whilst another engaged the enemy infantry columns now visible advancing down the shallow slopes towards them. The infantry of 55e Division de réserve formed a hurried line to the east of the villages of Iverny and Villeroy. But an attempted flanking movement by the Brigade Marocaine towards Penchard was bloodily repulsed with over 1,200 casualties. Lieutenant Alphonse Juin was then an officer in the Brigade Marocaine. He noted drily, 'We must learn to adapt.' Seeking to disengage the unfortunate Africans, the infantry of 55e Division de réserve advanced from Villeroy. But they were met with heavy enemy fire. Amongst those killed was the writer Charles Péguy, an officer serving with Ve/276e RI. One of his poems included the prophetic line, 'Happy are those who die in great battles.'

TOP
General Alexander von Linsingen (1850–1935), commander of II Armeekorps. Linsingen would spend most of the war on the Eastern Front, where he rose to command his own army group.

BOTTOM
The hill at Trocy, where much of the German reserve artillery was located. Just visible in the centre is the spire of the church at Etrépilly, showing how deeply the village is situated in its valley.

FRENCH FORCES

5e Groupe de divisions de réserve (*Général Beaudenom de Lamaze*)
55e Division de réserve (*Général Leguay*)
110e Brigade (*Général Malubray*)

1 Ve & VIe Bataillons, 231e Régiment d'infanterie
2 Ve & VIe Bataillons, 246e Régiment d'infanterie
3 Ve & VIe Bataillons, 276e Régiment d'infanterie
4 Groupe of three batteries, 13e Régiment d'artillerie
5 Groupe of three batteries, 30e Régiment d'artillerie
6 Groupe of three batteries, 45e Régiment d'artillerie

Brigade Marocaine (*Général Ditte*)

7 IVe & Ve Bataillons, 1er Régiment de chasseurs indigènes
8 Ier and IIe Bataillons, 2e Régiment de chasseurs indigènes

56e Division de réserve (*Général de Dartein*)
112e Brigade (*Général Cornille*)

9 Ve & VIe Bataillons, 350e Régiment d'Infanterie
10 Ve & VIe Bataillons, 361e Régiment d'Infanterie
11 65e Bataillon de chasseurs à pied
12 69e Bataillon de chasseurs à pied
13 Groupe of three batteries, 40e Régiment d'artillerie

▼ **EVENTS**

1 0715hrs: French cavalry reports Monthyon–Penchard area free of the enemy.

2 1100hrs: advancing German scouts reveal the presence of French forces, and the corps commander decides to attack. 7. Reserve-Division is sent to advance along the south edge of Saint-Soupplets Wood, clearing the wood at the same time; 22. Reserve-Division is sent to cover its left flank.

3 1200hrs: an artillery duel opens, as skirmishers deploy on both sides.

4 1330hrs: an attempt to hold the village of Saint-Soupplets by the 361e is foiled by the German advance, and the French are forced to withdraw into the wood. Supported by the two chasseur battalions, they manage to form, and hold, a line in the thick woodland.

5 1400hrs: an attempt by a company of VIe/276e to drive off the enemy artillery is driven back. The German artillery is obliged to withdraw out of range of the French guns.

6 1500hrs: the Brigade Marocaine advances through Chauconin and Neufmontiers, reaching Penchard, but is halted by artillery and small-arms fire. On the other flank, the 350e makes an attempt to recapture Saint-Soupplets, but is driven back without reaching any of its objectives.

7 1600hrs: the German counterattack by 44. Reserve-Brigade inflicts heavy casualties on the Moroccans, and they are forced to withdraw behind the village of Villeroy.

8 1630hrs: Ve/276e RI advances to cover the retreat of the Moroccans, but it too loses many men to German fire, and has to fall back in its turn. The 246e is in danger of being enveloped, and begins to withdraw. But the 231e advances and the French line is re-established.

9 1700hrs: the Germans advance to the line of the Ru de la Sorcière and hold all attempts by the French to dislodge them.

10 1800hrs: the French make another attempt to capture Saint-Soupplets, but are unable to cross the fields between the wood and the village.

11 1900hrs: another attempt is made to retake Saint-Soupplets by 65e BCP; it succeeds, but only because the Germans have withdrawn.

1930hrs: 'cease fire' is sounded. The Germans, concerned about their right flank, fall back during the night to better positions.

THE OPENING DAY OF THE BATTLE OF THE OURCQ, 5 SEPTEMBER 1914

Both French and German forces deploy from their lines of march in an unexpected and bloody encounter batt

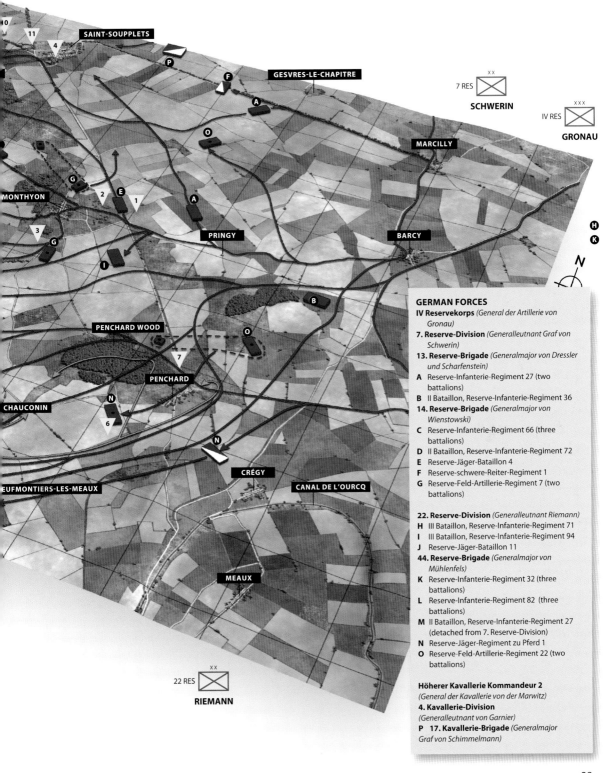

SAINT-SOUPPLETS

GESVRES-LE-CHAPITRE

7 RES
SCHWERIN

IV RES
GRONAU

MARCILLY

MONTHYON

PRINGY

BARCY

PENCHARD WOOD

PENCHARD

CHAUCONIN

CRÉGY

CANAL DE L'OURCQ

EUFMONTIERS-LES-MEAUX

MEAUX

22 RES
RIEMANN

GERMAN FORCES

IV Reservekorps (*General der Artillerie von Gronau*)

7. Reserve-Division (*Generalleutnant Graf von Schwerin*)

13. Reserve-Brigade (*Generalmajor von Dressler und Scharfenstein*)

A   Reserve-Infanterie-Regiment 27 (two battalions)
B   II Bataillon, Reserve-Infanterie-Regiment 36

14. Reserve-Brigade (*Generalmajor von Wienstowski*)

C   Reserve-Infanterie-Regiment 66 (three battalions)
D   II Bataillon, Reserve-Infanterie-Regiment 72
E   Reserve-Jäger-Bataillon 4
F   Reserve-schwere-Reiter-Regiment 1
G   Reserve-Feld-Artillerie-Regiment 7 (two battalions)

22. Reserve-Division (*Generalleutnant Riemann*)

H   III Bataillon, Reserve-Infanterie-Regiment 71
I   III Bataillon, Reserve-Infanterie-Regiment 94
J   Reserve-Jäger-Bataillon 11

44. Reserve-Brigade (*Generalmajor von Mühlenfels*)

K   Reserve-Infanterie-Regiment 32 (three battalions)
L   Reserve-Infanterie-Regiment 82 (three battalions)
M   II Bataillon, Reserve-Infanterie-Regiment 27 (detached from 7. Reserve-Division)
N   Reserve-Jäger-Regiment zu Pferd 1
O   Reserve-Feld-Artillerie-Regiment 22 (two battalions)

Höherer Kavallerie Kommandeur 2
(*General der Kavallerie von der Marwitz*)

4. Kavallerie-Division
(*Generalleutnant von Garnier*)

P   **17. Kavallerie-Brigade** (*Generalmajor Graf von Schimmelmann*)

33

Mildred Aldrich was an American civilian living some 8km (5 miles) distant, in a village south of the Marne. She paints a vivid picture of the action:

> The battle had advanced over the crest of the hill. The sun was shining brilliantly on Mareuil and Chauconin, but Monthyon and Penchard were enveloped in smoke. From the east and west we could see the artillery fire, but owing to the smoke hanging over the crest of the hill on the horizon, it was impossible to get an idea of the positions of the armies... the Germans were... to be pushed east, in which case the artillery to the west must either be the French or the English. The hard thing to bear was all that guesswork. There was only noise, belching smoke, and long drifts of white clouds concealing the hill.

Further north the advanced posts of 56e Division de réserve were forced to withdraw from Saint-Soupplets towards the wood of Tillières. Then a follow-up attack by RIR 27 (7. Reserve-Division) resulted in confused and bitter fighting in the wood itself. 14e Division d'infanterie (7e Corps d'armée), arriving in the midst of this mayhem, found itself thrown straight into action, moving towards Bouillancy in an attempt to locate the German flank.

That evening Gronau took stock. Concerned for his right flank, he decided his losses had been too great – and his consumption of ammunition too high – to continue his attack for a second day. He therefore issued orders to withdraw, taking up a position with his back to the Ourcq and with both flanks secure. At the same time he contacted Kluck to ask for help. His commander responded immediately. II Armeekorps (Linsingen) was closest to Gronau and was sent back across the Marne to his assistance.

6 September

Just before dawn, French patrols made a cautious entry into the village of Monthyon, but they found only stragglers and wounded. The Germans had withdrawn. Carrying on over the ridge that had formed their objective the previous day, the French moved down the other side towards the Multien Plateau. This was rolling countryside, crossed by several streams in deep, brush-filled valleys, but otherwise providing little cover. Most of the land was in cultivation, either cereals or sugar beet. The cereal had been gathered in, but the beet harvest was just about to begin. A number of large, walled farmhouses studded the countryside – many including small factory buildings for beet processing. The area was dominated by the hills at Penchard and Monthyon in the west, and by a low ridge between the Thérouanne and Gergogne streams to the north-east. Gronau had designated the western edge of the plateau as his defence line and placed his command post at Saint-Féron farm, near Trocy-en-Multien.

Clashes between the two advanced guards began around 1000hrs. The 56e Division de réserve was ordered to advance towards Saint-Soupplets and Forfry; 55e Division de réserve towards Marcilly and Barcy; and 45e Division d'infanterie towards Penchard and Chambry. 7e Corps d'armée was to attack the Multien Ridge. By midday an artillery duel had intensified and close action was imminent.

Just then elements of II Armeekorps began to arrive on the scene. Setting up his headquarters at Beauval, just east of Trocy-en-Multien, Linsingen quickly grasped what the French were trying to do and split his force accordingly. 3. Infanterie-Division was ordered to take its place opposite the French right at Varreddes. Meanwhile 4. Infanterie-Division was sent to the opposite flank, to Rosoy-en-Multien, to counter the French turning movement.

But the new arrivals had not gone unnoticed by French aerial reconnaissance, and Maunoury took immediate action. Quick to perceive the threat now facing his right, he reinforced the attacks of 55e and 56e Divisions de réserve with 45e Division d'infanterie and ordered the newcomers to be 'thrown into the Marne'.

289e RI (109e Brigade, 55e Division) was made up of men who lived in this very area. They had found the previous day particularly hard. Passing through the village of Iverny, for example, some were shocked to see their own homes in flames – the whereabouts of their families unknown. Their comrades in 110e Brigade were also in a difficult position. They had taken heavy casualties on 5 September and had exhausted almost all their small-arms ammunition. But, before they had time to resupply, they were thrust back into the firing line. Their brigadier, Général de Mainbray, is reported to have taken one look at the open, featureless plain his men were to cross and wept. Throughout a long hot afternoon, the French tried again and again to reach the German lines. Units and sub-units coalesced into an 'immense line of riflemen deployed [in an] irregular chain, sinuous in appearance, formed of links so closely attached that a movement at one end [rippled] down in waves to the other'. By 1630hrs they could do no more – 246e RI, for example, had lost nearly 600 men – and they withdrew to Barcy.

It was a similar story for 56e Division de réserve before Etrépilly, and for the 45e and the Moroccans at Chambry. Much blood had been spilt but no progress made. With only one exception the Germans were content to remain within their defences. A counterattack against 56e Division de réserve was launched from the village of Etrépilly around 1700hrs, but this was broken up by four 75s firing over open sights at a range of 800m (875 yards).

On the French left, 14e Division d'infanterie and 63e Division de réserve were no more successful in their attempts to turn the German flank. The 14e had managed to establish itself in Acy-en-Multien. But a vigorous counterattack by 4. Infanterie-Division, supported by some battalions from 7. Reserve-Division, first stopped the French advance and then drove it back, recapturing Acy. For Leutnant Behrig, battalion adjutant of II./IR 14, the German counterattack was 'like a battle picture from 1870… hundreds of men charging forward, hundreds cheering at the tops of their voices'. Driving in the German pickets, 63e Division de réserve had more success. It captured Champfleury Farm and the village of Puisieux after a bitter struggle. But, in the face of German fire, it could not cross the open ground to the east.

LEFT
The centre of the village of Barcy. From here 55e Division d'infanterie mounted a series of fruitless assaults on the position of 3. Infanterie-Division above Varreddes.

RIGHT
Looking across a beet field towards the German positions at Varreddes, marked by the distant line of trees (centre). On 6 September the men of 55e Division d'infanterie strove in vain to cross these fields under withering fire.

THE TAXIS OF THE MARNE (pp. 36–37)

Using taxis was an exceptional piece of improvization on the part of Général Gallieni. By the evening of 6 September, the men of 7e Division d'infanterie had been travelling for 12 days, and were in no condition to march a further 60km (37 miles) to the front at Nanteuil. But it was vital to get them there as quickly as possible. Using his powers as military governor of Paris, Gallieni requisitioned 1,200 local taxis (**1**), which assembled outside the Invalides that afternoon. Most were 12hp Renault AG or AG-1, although there were also some Panhards, Clément-Bayards and Peugeots. Picking up men of 103e and 104e Rls (**2**) in Livry, on the outskirts of Paris, around 1900hrs, they reached their destination around 0200hrs the following morning. They then turned round and formed a second convoy, transporting the remainder of the two regiments. The effort was not without its problems. Some drivers ignored convoy discipline, overtaking others in an effort to get to their destination quickly. Others diverted from the route in order to get a little food or drink for their passengers – such was the hurry to get the men to the front that no food had been issued that morning – and had to be returned to the convoy by police. The taxi drivers (**3**), all aged over 50, and working for some 40 hours with only short breaks, returned to their depots to work out the bill. Tariff number 2 (more than two persons outside the city boundaries) was 75 centimes for the first 750m (820 yards) and a further 10 centimes for each extra 250m (270 yards), of which the driver received 27 per cent. The French Treasury paid out 70,102 francs altogether. After their heroic efforts on 6–7 September, taxis continued to play a part in the battle. They were used to return officers to their units (in one case coming under fire), and on 8 and 15 September to evacuate the wounded.

Yet the French had succeeded in weakening their opponents. Morale, especially in IV Reservekorps, was very low indeed. Evening enabled both sides to take stock, and Linsingen once again contacted Kluck. He needed more support, preferably by first light. 'The battle along the line Etavigny–north of Varreddes has only halted the enemy by extensive artillery fire. Since IV Reservekorps has suffered the loss of much of its fighting strength, and II Armeekorps is facing superior numbers, it is vital that IV Armeekorps should intervene by 0500hrs.'

Kluck obliged at once, ordering IV Armeekorps to turn round and join the German forces on the Ourcq. At the same time, he moved his HQ to be nearer the battle – from Rebais, south of the Marne, first to Charly-sur-Marne, and then north again to Vendrest, above the Ourcq Valley. General Arnim, commanding IV Armeekorps, arrived at Linsingen's headquarters at 0200hrs on 7 September. The two men now devised a plan for the coming day. Like II Armeekorps, IV Armeekorps would be split. 7. Infanterie-Division would go to join 4. Infanterie-Division in the north, moving to the extreme right to forestall and if possible outflank the French flanking movements. Meanwhile 8. Infanterie-Division was to bolster IV Reservekorps. 3. Infanterie-Division, positioned on the outside of a loop of the Ourcq, under French artillery fire and with its rear towards the advancing BEF, would have to look after itself. Linsingen would take command of the southern sector of the defences; Arnim, the northern.

Meanwhile Kluck was still taking stock of his situation. Two corps now remained south of the Marne – III Armeekorps (Lochow) and IX Armeekorps (Quast). At 2100hrs he ordered them to halt in their current positions and placed them under the temporary command of 2. Armee. But later that night he changed his mind. Still mindful of the problems facing his right, he recalled both corps and ordered them to march north immediately. This would leave a dangerous gap between his left flank and the right of 2. Armee. But Kluck remained unconcerned. In his view, he still had plenty of time to overcome the French opposite him, before resuming his march south-eastwards and going on to defeat 5e Armée.

Champfleury Farm from the south. The farm dominates the approaches to Etrépilly, which lies just off the photo to the right.

Höherer Kavallerie-Kommandeur 2 (Marwitz) was now the only formation remaining at Kluck's disposal. And Marwitz's men were no longer at full strength. 4. Kavallerie-Division was already involved in the fighting on the Ourcq, leaving only 2. and 9. Kavallerie-Divisionen to cover 1. Armee's left flank.

7 September

Reinforcements were also arriving on the French side as the various regiments making up 4e Corps d'armée began to reach the Paris stations, though they were worn out by the fighting they had experienced in the east and by their five-day train journey. Their commander requested they be given 48 hours' rest to recover. Out of the question, came Gallieni's reply. The corps was immediately split up and its two divisions allotted to different sectors of the front. 8e Division d'infanterie was to head south of Meaux, to serve as a link with the advancing BEF. Meanwhile, the men of 7e Division d'infanterie were needed to reinforce the left of 6e Armée – 50km (31 miles) away. But one problem remained. How to get them there?

A railway went part of the way, as far as Crépy-en-Valois. But recent sightings of German troops in the neighbourhood had led to fears that the track had been sabotaged. Just a few days earlier, the government had requisitioned all the taxis in Paris. Might they provide the answer? The taxis – and their drivers – were quickly called together and the men clambered aboard. Space was limited – with four men crammed inside each vehicle and one more in the luggage compartment – so in the event only 103e and 104e RIs travelled in this way. And the taxi drivers, though willing, had no idea of convoy discipline. With units and sub-units arriving mixed up, it took precious hours to restore a semblance of order. Nevertheless, the heroic intervention of the 'taxis of the Marne' quickly seized the popular imagination and became the enduring image of the battle.

Meanwhile the Germans had reorganized themselves into three battlegroups under the overall command of Linsingen: the Nordgruppe under Arnim, consisting of 4. and 7. Infanterie-Divisionen, plus 16. Infanterie-Brigade; the Mittelgruppe under Gronau (8. Infanterie-Division, less 16. Infanterie-Brigade, and 7. Reserve-Division); and the Südgruppe under Generalleutnant von Trossel (Trossel's own 3. Infanterie-Division and 22. Reserve-Division).

As the early morning mist cleared, the French resumed their attacks. In a day of see-saw action, 45e Division d'infanterie tried once again to cross the fields to the east of Chambry, only to be stopped in its tracks by German artillery and small-arms fire. The village of Puisieux was held, but only thanks to the intervention of five batteries of 5e RA, commanded by Colonel Robert Nivelle. Firing over open sights, their guns succeeded in breaking up a German counterattack. Following this rebuff, the Germans chose once more not to press and resumed their positions. A determined attack from IR 32 drove 63e Division de réserve away from Nogeon Farm. But the French quickly countered, retook the farm and captured one of IR 32's colours into the bargain.

Further north 14e Division d'infanterie was pressed back further by enemy attacks, but the Germans could not break through. At Betz, 61e Division de réserve tried to work its way around the German flank. Defending the village were the men of 7. Infanterie-Division. Newly arrived after a 60km (37-mile) approach march, they nevertheless gave a good account of themselves and the French were driven back in some disorder towards Nanteuil-le-Haudouin. The Corps de cavalerie then organized an old-fashioned raid – 5e Division de cavalerie was sent to attack across the rear of the German right flank. But this failed to produce any noticeable slackening in the overall pressure.

In the centre Etrépilly was once again the main focus of attention. Situated in a shallow valley, it controlled access to the hill behind Trocy, where much of the German reserve artillery was stationed. The village itself was held by II./RIR 32, with the three battalions of RIR 82 – the other regiment of the brigade – positioned just to the north. During the course of the afternoon the Germans made several attempts to advance westwards. But on each occasion they were driven back by small-arms and artillery fire. As evening fell they were still in the village – tired, hungry, thirsty and discouraged.

Suddenly, from the west, their advance posts were driven in by an attack from 2e bis Zouaves. The defenders panicked and a crowd of men – French and German – rushed through the main street. A second attack by 350e and 294e RIs now came from the north-west. This forced the Germans to withdraw still further from the centre of the village and eventually to abandon it altogether. But senior officers, including the brigadier and the regimental commander, halted their hasty retreat with pistols drawn.

Night had now fallen and the Germans tried to re-enter the village by the light of burning hayricks. The *zouaves* had lost their commanding officer and many of their men in a desperate firefight around the cemetery. So, fearful of being cut off and surrounded in the dark, the French withdrew. And, after driving off the enemy, so too did the Germans.

LEFT
The interior of Nogeon Farm some months after the battle. On the right the chimney marks the small beet-processing factory common to many farms in the area. The farms were all solidly built with thick walls placed around a courtyard, making them ideal for defence.

RIGHT
Outside the main gate of Nogeon Farm.

That same evening another surprise attack was launched – this time by the Brigade Marocaine – against the left wing of 3. Infanterie-Division, around Varreddes. The division remained in a precarious situation, occupying the edge of the plateau above the village and the canalized river Ourcq – with the advancing British somewhere to the rear. Again the sudden attack led to panic among some of the defenders. But, rallying to the call of the 'Enemy Broken Through', a scratch force of men from four different units, infantry and artillery, succeeded in driving off the attackers.

8 September

At dawn on 8 September, French artillery opened fire on the positions of the German artillery reserve, 24 batteries strong, at Trocy. Faced with yet another attack, Gronau was unsure whether the battered units of IV Reservekorps would be able to resist 'a noticeably stronger enemy'. His corps had no reserves, 'having spent the whole day under a hot sun without water or food, waiting in vain either to be relieved or reinforced'. The regimental cookers and baggage had failed to join up with their parent units. The rear areas were clogged with wounded and stragglers, and the smoke from burning hayricks mingled with the smell from the corpses – of men and horses – blocking the nearby streams. In the event Gronau's fears went unrealized. The French, exhausted by the effort of the previous few days, were unable to press any attacks. In the evening 5. Infanterie-Division arrived from the Marne. Worn out by its exertions, it nevertheless went straight into the line to support IV Reservekorps.

But Gronau's men were not the only ones who were suffering. The continuous action was taking its toll right across the German lines. In mid-morning 3. Infanterie-Division pulled back from the heights above Varreddes, creating a shortened line to the south of Etrépilly, between the village and the Ourcq. The division was certainly exhausted, but the threat posed by the advancing BEF also played its part. So too did the imminent loss of a regiment to act as flank guard.

Further north 7e Division d'infanterie was fully assembled behind French lines by early morning. But no move was made to send it on a flanking mission around the German right. Instead it was simply fed into the line to the south of 61e Division de réserve – replacing losses rather than providing a decisive intervention. During the morning 7e Division d'infanterie made progress towards the village of Etavigny, whilst 61e Division de réserve secured Montrolles Wood. But at nightfall the forward units of the 61e withdrew and units of 7e Division d'infanterie were forced to follow suit. Attempts by the Corps de cavalerie to find the German right flank were brushed aside. An evening thunderstorm put paid to combat for the day.

216e RI, made up of reservists from the Massif Central, had found the past three days of fighting very hard:

> The lines of riflemen that manoeuvred with such precision were brought to earth by machine-gun fire. Losses were severe. Almost all the senior officers were out of action. Despite this, the regiment tried to advance. But the enemy, concealed behind the banks alongside a main road, forced them to ground every time with horrific machine gun fire. Then the 'coalboxes', with their dreadful noise and huge craters, wore down nerves that were already frayed to breaking point. Damn these fields of beetroot!... Five officers were killed, sixteen wounded. And to cap it all, our 75s took no notice of where we were and shelled our advanced positions, which removed all our urgency in continuing

the attack. Fortunately, night fell. What was left of the regiment fell back several hundred metres in the rear, illuminated by the fires of burning houses and hayricks. Half the regiment were casualties. The Supply Officer, Lieutenant Monneyron, brought up some food, but no-one could be bothered to set to and cook it. Only some tobacco was welcome. Worn out by three days of fighting, the regiment fell into the sleep of the dead.

216e RI had begun the battle with a total of 3,202 men and 37 officers; that evening only 1,146 men and 14 officers remained to answer the roll.

Disappointed with the facilities at Vendrest, Kluck decided to move his headquarters again – this time to La Ferté-Milon, a further 15km (9 miles) to the north. Just short of the town, French cavalry, for once taking the offensive, ambushed his convoy. Only the timely arrival of an infantry battalion, which drove the French off, allowed Kluck to reach his headquarters in safety.

Joffre had by now decided that 6e Armée was incapable of maintaining its push towards Château-Thierry. III and IX Armeekorps were reinforcing 1. Armee, and troops released by the fall of Maubeuge on 7 September would soon be arriving as well. But 6e Armée still had an important role to play: keeping up the pressure on the Germans to draw their attention away from the advances of the BEF and 5e Armée. Meanwhile Maunoury prepared for the worst – a strong German counterattack – by readying a final defensive line along the line of higher ground Plessis–Belleville–Monthyon–Penchard.

9 September
By the morning of 9 September the whole of III Armeekorps had completed its march from the Marne – a journey of over 80km (50 miles) in two days. 5. Infanterie-Division had immediately gone to bolster the tired units of IV Reservekorps. 6. Infanterie-Division now marched off to the right flank. Walter Bloem, commanding 2./Gren.R. 12 later recalled the exertions of the march:

> It was impossible to keep a proper order of march... the whole company [was] dislocated. You scold, you admonish, you try to crack a joke. No response, not a sound, not a smile: neither laughter nor grumbling. Spirits are rock-bottom, and there is only the monotonous tramp of blistered feet, tired to death. And so it went on for hour after hour. Whoever asked this of the men knew he was asking the impossible. There must [have been] a lot, no, everything, resting on it.

Although they had further to march, the men of IX Armeekorps were not that far behind and soon took up their place on the right. Kluck's orders for the day began, 'Tomorrow the decisive action will take place with an enveloping attack by the northern wing (IX Armeekorps, 6. Infanterie-Division and 4. Kavallerie-Division) from the direction of Cuvergnon.'

The blow expected by Maunoury came early in the morning. Both divisions of IX Armeekorps, with 6. Infanterie-Division under command, attacked the positions of 61e Division de réserve, and the French were driven back in some disorder. With the sudden withdrawal of the 61e, 7e Division d'infanterie had to fall back as well. Eventually the intermingled regiments of the two divisions managed to form a precarious defensive line.

Later that morning the French were attacked from a different quarter, with the arrival of Brigade Lepel (43. Reserve-Brigade, 22. Reserve Division) – troops released from lines of communication duties in Brussels. Going straight into action from the line of march, the brigade brushed aside the 315e and 317e, the

After the battle Moroccan *chasseurs* gather in front of the church at Neufmontiers to sort through abandoned German equipment in search of souvenirs.

two reserve regiments posted as flank guards, and threatened the flank of the retreating 61e Division de réserve. Reaching as far as Nanteuil-le-Haudouin, elements of the brigade cut the main road south of the town, provoking panic amongst the rear echelon troops there. Once again the French artillery saved the day. Two groups of 44e RA engaged the enemy over open sights around Chèvreville, and once again the German attack broke up.

Kluck urged speed on his commanders. He aimed to deal first with Maunoury before wheeling again to tackle the BEF, coming up from the south. But events were beginning to escape his control. He was obliged to pull back his southernmost units – 3., 4. and 8. Infanterie-Divisionen, and 7. and 22. Reserve-Divisionen – to protect his left flank against the threat posed by the BEF.

1ère Division de cavalerie launched a tentative movement against the German flank, and this seemed to be enough for Lepel. He withdrew northwards around 1800hrs to avoid encirclement, and the French cavalry did not press the point.

The French line was now bent at right angles with its left in the air. Abandoning attempts to maintain a link with the BEF, 8e Division d'infanterie was recalled to block the road to Paris. Gallieni scraped together what he could of the troops remaining in the capital to provide Maunoury with further reinforcements. But it would not be sufficient. The men of 6e Armée had suffered very heavy losses and were exhausted. The German attack expected at dawn on 10 September would be enough to send Maunoury's troops into headlong retreat, and Paris would be lost.

Heavy action in the fighting around Nogeon Farm had reduced 60e RI to just 12 officers and 926 men, commanded by a captain. That evening, one officer recalled, 'after five days and nights of fighting, [we were] decimated, exhausted, starving. We threw ourselves down on some open ground, having nothing else left inside us other than the knowledge that in the morning we would have to obey the order to either advance or die where we stood.'

But the attack he was expecting never came. Patrols reported that the German positions were empty and the enemy in retreat. There was little the French infantry could do to stop them. But the cavalry did move forward and captured another enemy colour. At Mont-l'Evêque, near Senlis, a captain of 3e Hussars succeeded in taking the colour of Ldw.IR 94.

The battle of the Saint-Gond Marshes, 6–9 September 1914

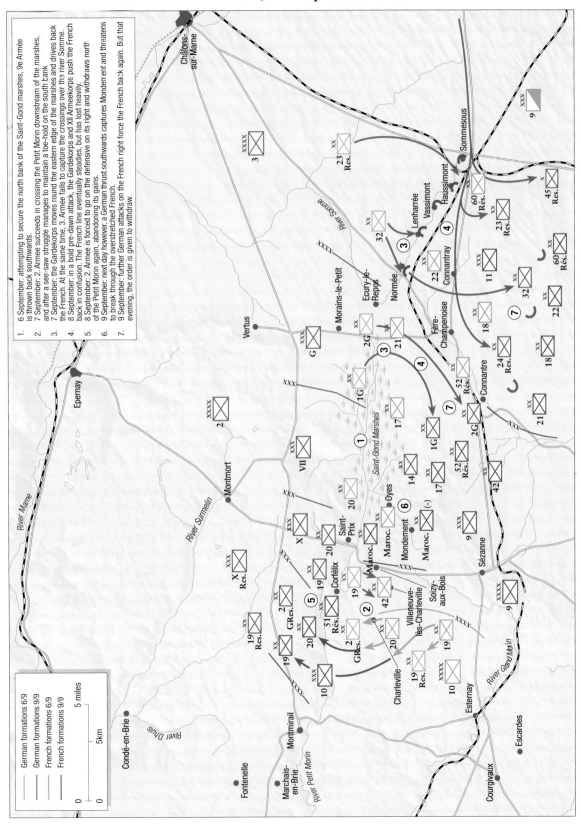

1. 6 September: attempting to secure the north bank of the Saint-Gond marshes, 9e Armée is thrown back southwards.
2. 7 September: 2. Armee succeeds in crossing the Petit Morin downstream of the marshes, and after a see-saw struggle manages to maintain a toe-hold on the south bank
3. 7 September: the Gardekorps moves round the eastern edge of the marshes and drives back the French. At the same time, 3. Armee fails to capture the crossings over the river Somme.
4. 8 September: in a bold pre-dawn attack, the Gardekorps and XII Armeekorps push the French back in confusion. The French line eventually steadies, but has lost heavily.
5. 8 September: 2. Armee is forced to go on the defensive on its right and withdraws north of the Petit Morin again, abandoning its gains.
6. 9 September: next day however, a German thrust southwards captures Mondement and threatens to break through the overstretched French.
7. 9 September: further German attacks on the French right force the French back again. But that evening, the order is given to withdraw.

45

THE BATTLE OF THE SAINT-GOND MARSHES, 6–10 SEPTEMBER

Général Foch, commander of 9e Armée. As a former director of the French staff college, Foch helped lay the theoretical groundwork for the army's offensive spirit. He placed particular emphasis on the will to fight – 'a battle is only lost when you believe it lost'. But another general caustically remarked that Foch 'knew nothing of the practicalities of combat'.

While Kluck raced ahead on the German right, Moltke had wider concerns. Reports were coming in of a British landing at Ostend and of the dispatch of a Russian corps to Britain. Both would threaten his lines of communication. Moltke decided to increase the pressure on the French positions around Verdun, in another attempt to unhinge the French lines. He also planned to transfer 7. Armee to Belgium. But for the moment he was unable to disengage.

Général Sarrail, who had replaced Ruffey as commander of 3e Armée, was determined to hold on to the fortress town of Verdun. For Joffre, however, Verdun was of secondary importance. Like Paris, it was just one town. Joffre was more concerned about the integrity of his line as a whole. 5. Armee succeeded in crossing the Meuse, but their advance was held up by the ring of forts around Verdun. Meanwhile their comrades in 4. Armee could make little headway in terms of ground. But the overall pressure exerted by the Germans drew more and more elements of 4e Armée into battle. The result was a gap, some 20km (12 miles) wide, in the centre of the French line, between 4e and 5e Armées.

With no strategic reserve, Joffre had to look elsewhere to find the men to plug the breach. He took two corps (9e and 11e) from 4e Armée and added more troops from 1ère Armée – 9e Division de cavalerie, plus a division that had been serving in Morocco when war broke out. Command of this newly created 9e Armée was given to Général Ferdinand Foch, the commander of 20e Corps d'armée.

Opposing Foch were elements from 2. and 3. Armeen, both of them weakened by the demands of the Belgian and Eastern fronts. 2. Armee had lost VII Reservekorps to the siege of Maubeuge and the Garde-Reservekorps as reinforcements to East Prussia. 3. Armee had lost 24. Reserve-Division to the siege of Givet and XI Armeekorps to the Russian Front. 3. Armee found itself in a particularly invidious position. Repeatedly called upon to support its neighbouring armies, 2. and 4., it had been unable to impose any consistent pressure on the French.

The terrain occupied by 9e Armée fell into three distinct sections. To the west lay the Brie Plateau. This was rolling, heavily wooded countryside, cut – some 80m (262ft) below the level of the plateau itself – by the steep-sided, winding valley of the Petit Morin. Further east the ground rose to form several ridges, marking the boundary of the Paris basin. The southernmost, Allemant Ridge, was a key point, offering views in both directions – northwards towards the Petit Morin and southwards towards the Seine. To the north, the ridges created a natural amphitheatre. This enclosed a plain that included several isolated hills, such as Mont Août and Mont-Aimé, and also the formidable obstacle of the Saint-Gond marshes, extending on either side of the Petit Morin.

Attempts had been made to drain the marshes, and the land was criss-crossed by drainage ditches that fed into canalized streams. But, in 1914, they were still sizeable – some 3km (2 miles) wide and 19km (12 miles) long. Although it was possible to make progress across country in dry weather, heavy rain could soon reduce the fields to a quagmire. Three roads and five trackways, built up on causeways, provided the only routes across the marshes. But all were unmetalled and they too could very quickly turn to mud.

To the east of the ridges lay the start of the Champagne plain. This was virtually flat country, studded with pine copses, with poor soil and few watercourses. Among these were the Somme (not the river later to become so well known to the BEF), the Vaure and the Maurienne. Some writers would later claim that this was the area of the '*champs Catalauniques*', where Attila and his army of Huns had suffered defeat in AD 450. The parallel between these two decisive battles – an army from the east defeated by an army made up largely of Franks – made the comparison too good to resist.

On 4 September Moltke ordered the change of direction in the German advance that would see 1. and 2. Armeen deployed as flank guards. 2. Armee (Bülow) was to take up a position between the Marne and the Seine facing south-westwards. However, 3. Armee (Hausen) was to continue its advance, heading towards Troyes and Vendoeuvre. German patrols were just 50km (31 miles) from Paris.

On 5 September Joffre sent orders to his army commanders to resume the offensive. 9e Armée was to hold its ground. Meanwhile 5e Armée, 6e Armée and the BEF were to advance, turning the German flank and rolling up the whole of the enemy line. 9e Armée was disposed along a 20km (12-mile) front beside the Petit Morin and the Somme, guarding the southern exits from the Saint-Gond marshes and the western end of the Champagne plain. Nevertheless, it proved impossible to close up completely with 4e Armée. Just one cavalry division had to suffice to fill the gap between the right flank of the 9e and the left flank of the 4e. Foch reacted to his essentially defensive orders by throwing out advanced posts on the north side of the marshes.

6 September

To Foch's left the French were on the offensive; 5e Armée was already marching northwards into the gap in the German front created when II Armeekorps withdrew to the Ourcq. But to his front the situation was very different. Here 2. Armee had already advanced across the Petit Morin, and 10e Corps d'armée (Desforges) collided with X Reservekorps around the village of Charleville, south-east of Montmirail.

When 20e Division d'infanterie tried to bypass Charleville to the west, it was halted by 2. Garde-Reserve-Division. To their right the struggle for Charleville itself would involve elements from four different regiments and two different divisions – 20e and 42e – as the village was lost and then recaptured by 9e Armée. The neighbouring community of Villeneuve-lès-Charleville was the focus of a similar struggle – 151e RI losing and recapturing the village three times in the course of the afternoon. Further east the fighting was equally fierce. The Hanoverians of 19. Infanterie-Division made a vigorous assault on the rest of the front occupied by 42e Division d'infanterie. Meanwhile a similar see-saw struggle ensued for Branle Wood and the village of Soizy-aux-Bois. However, the Germans were prevented from advancing further by French artillery, and they spent the night of 6–7 September in the woods on the south side of the river.

The French sustained heavy losses in all these actions. In asking why, Général Grossetti (42e Division d'infanterie) identified faults that perhaps should have been remedied in pre-war manoeuvres: 'In today's attacks, our infantry were hit two or three times by our own artillery, and equally suffered severe losses that could have been prevented, because of [our] failure to prepare the attack with artillery fire, and [our] use of formations that were far too dense... numerous platoons stood shoulder-to-shoulder without any intervals. Two companies were deployed where one would have been sufficient.'

The village of Corfélix, looking eastwards up the valley of the Petit Morin, remained relatively unscathed, considering that 19. Infanterie-Division had mounted its attacks on Soizy through the village.

In Charleville the situation of the French was so exposed that Desforges gave his brigadier (Général Cadoudal, 40e Brigade) permission to withdraw. But Cadoudal was implacable in his response to the hapless staff officer who brought the message. 'How could I dare evacuate [a] position,' he retorted, 'that has so resisted the enemy, abandoning the bodies of the men who sacrificed themselves to hold it? Tell Général Desforges that I am staying in Charleville, and he will find me here, no matter what.'

On the French right flank the Bretons of 11e Corps d'armée (Eydoux) were playing an entirely defensive role. They dug in along the line of the Somme to control the crossing points on the river, taking up positions between the villages of Morains-le-Petit and Lenharrée, with isolated battalions further south-eastwards, as far as the railway junction at Sommesous. At the northern end of their front, the men of 2. Garde-Infanterie-Division were doing better than their comrades in 1. Garde-Infanterie-Division. They managed to force 21e Division d'infanterie out of many of its positions during the afternoon. And by evening the French had lost control of the neck of land between the marshes and the Somme. Further south Général Eydoux was scrambling to put the rest of his battalions into some kind of defensive order. But he met with little success. The front was too long to hold comfortably with the two divisions of regulars and one of reservists available to him.

To the west 9e Corps d'armée (Dubois) threw men across the marshes to hold the northern end of the crossings. But there he encountered troops from 20. Infanterie-Division and the Gardekorps (Plettenberg) coming south. With insufficient support from their own artillery – which, for the most part, remained south of the marshes – the French battalions took heavy casualties and made no gains. The two regiments most heavily engaged – 77e and 135e RIs – each lost around 500 men. By afternoon 9e Corps d'armée was back on the south side of the marshes. The Gardekorps now moved off to its left to find a way around the eastern end of the marshes. But here they found greater opposition. Heavy artillery fire stopped the advance of 1. Garde-Infanterie-Division in its tracks, and Plettenberg turned to the neighbouring XII Armeekorps (d'Elsa) for support.

A grave at Soizy-aux-Bois, containing the remains of men of 162e RI. The regiment, whose peacetime depot was Verdun, lost ten officers and 814 men during the battle. Altogether 395 Frenchmen and 333 Germans were killed within the boundaries of the commune; the parish clergy would bury most of them.

General Hausen, commanding 3. Armee, had ordered a rest day for 5 September, so most of his men were slightly behind those of 2. Armee. General d'Elsa could hear gunfire from the west – the Gardekorps going into action around Morains-le-Petit. When asked to help them find the French flank he was quick to oblige and sent 32. Infanterie-Division (Planitz) to assist. Planitz had already launched his own attack against the French-held villages of Normée and Lenharrée, but had been driven back by French artillery. Hausen took great satisfaction in the parallel with 1870: 'As at St Privat [when a timely attack by the Saxon Corps had saved the Prussian Guard from decimation] the Guard were helped by the Saxons.'

The Garde were not the only ones looking to 3. Armee for help: 4. Armee too was seeking support. Once again, Hausen reacted positively. Confident that he was dealing with nothing more than an affair of outposts, and that the French would continue their retreat as far as the Seine, he sent 23. Reserve-Division to assist. But his action virtually divided 3. Armee into two wings, some 30km (19 miles) apart.

By nightfall neither army had achieved all its objectives. The German advance had blocked Foch's move northwards. But, at the same time, a desperate French defence had thwarted the German advance. The result was stalemate, with the French still controlling the southern exits to the marshes and much of the high ground to the south of the Petit Morin.

7 September

Despite the setbacks of the previous day, Foch saw no reason to put an end to his attacks. The role of 9e Armée was to support 5e Armée in its offensive. And, for Foch, this was a task best achieved by continuing to attack – so drawing enemy troops away from Franchet d'Esperey's advance. On the right 11e Corps d'armée was to hold its positions on the Somme before counterattacking – first north-westwards and then northwards towards Pierre-Morains and Mont-Aimé. To their left 9e Corps d'armée was to defend the exits from the marshes and then conform with the advance of the 11e. On the left 42e Division d'infanterie was to act as the link between 9e and 5e Armées, supporting the right flank of 10e Corps d'armée.

On the German side, the sudden withdrawal of II and IV Armeekorps back to the Ourcq left Bülow's right flank in the air. He therefore decided to go on the defensive in that sector, using III and IX Armeekorps – the two 1. Armee formations placed under his command by Kluck – to guard his flank. On the left – where he would ask 3. Armee to continue to support the Gardekorps – attacks would carry on.

On the French left, 42e Division d'infanterie received the order to evacuate the isolated post of Villeneuve-lès-Charleville, and completed the operation without attracting German attention. But they had scarcely regained their own lines when they were ordered to retake Villeneuve once more. Supported by the divisional and corps artillery, 151e RI managed to re-establish a toehold in the village, but the German counter-bombardment ensured it would remain no more than that. In response to the renewed assault on Villeneuve, the Germans attacked once more towards Soizy-aux-Bois.

The French troops at Soizy, 162e RI, faced a particularly difficult task. As the right flank of 42e Division d'infanterie, their role was to hold the village without losing contact with the Division Marocaine on their right. But the pressure exerted by the Germans was too great, and 162e RI was forced to fall back to the hills south of the village. 20e Division d'infanterie now tried to find the German flank. Attacking towards Bout-de-la-Ville, it created enough space for 51e Division de réserve to deploy its artillery to cover the French front before Branle Wood. Counterattack followed counterattack in the wood until the front had stabilized. Nevertheless, Soizy, scarcely 10km (6 miles) north of the town of Sézanne, remained in German hands. And if the Germans could capture Sézanne, they would be in a position to divide 5e and 9e Armées, and go on to destroy them in detail.

9e Corps d'armée was ordered to defend the Mondement–Allemant Ridge sector and maintain French domination of the Saint-Gond crossings. Following the fall of Soizy, the Division Marocaine – on the left of 9e Corps d'armée – quickly came under pressure from 19. Infanterie-Division, which then went on to clear the French from the Crête du Poirier, a spur dominating the western end of the marshes. Foch ordered 42e Division d'infanterie and the Division Marocaine to counterattack. The attack was to begin at 1445hrs – its aim to recapture the spur and the village of Saint-Prix beyond. But the

French publishers, desperate to publish images of the conflict, were not above faking photographs of the action. Here running men, perhaps photographed on pre-war manoeuvres, are superimposed upon a picture of a shelled village.

difficulties of assembling the men and getting them to the start line in the blazing heat of late summer proved too much. There was insufficient time that day for artillery preparation and the attack was postponed.

In the east the Gardekorps moved to the left to throw its full weight against the positions held by 11e Corps d'armée in the Morains-le-Petit–Ecury sector. However, the open nature of the countryside meant concealment was difficult and a heavy artillery bombardment met every German forward movement. The villages along the Somme each changed hands several times during the day. But that evening the men of the Gardekorps had to bivouac back on their start line. On the left the Saxons had met with a similar fate. Unable to cross the Somme, their attempt to outflank the French via Sommesous had also ended in failure.

The Germans were in an increasingly precarious situation. All formations were extremely tired – worn out by the constant pressure of marching and fighting since 20 August – and the French artillery was managing to hold all their attempts to advance further. And, with the Gardekorps moving to its left to skirt the marshes, a significant gap had developed in 2. Armee's front – between the Gardekorps and X Armeekorps to their right. As a result, the German grip on that sector of the north bank of the Petit Morin – now held by nothing more than a few isolated companies and squadrons – was tenuous. Neither X Armeekorps nor the Gardekorps could do anything. With every available man needed in the front line, they had no one to spare. Bülow had no alternative but to detach 14. Infanterie-Division from his reserve to fill the gap.

For Hausen, the key to victory lay in mounting a concerted attack to rupture the French line at its weakest point. 'The enemy cannot be strong everywhere', he explained. 'An attack at his weakest point will result in a breakthrough and, at the very least, act to relieve the pressure on the German right.' His plan was to launch an attack before dawn – without artillery preparation – surprising the French and also nullifying their advantage in firepower. The Gardekorps and XII Armeekorps would attack on the right, while the remainder of 3. Armee and some 4. Armee units were deployed on the left. Some of the divisional commanders were dismayed at the thought of yet another assault: their men needed rest. But Bülow and the Herzog von Württemberg (4. Armee) supported Hausen's proposal.

8 September

The attack began at 0330hrs. The main assault was launched by a battlegroup three divisions strong – 2. Garde-Infanterie-Division, 32. Infanterie-Division and 23. Reserve-Division – under the overall command of General der Artillerie Kirchbach. Battalions from all four Garde regiments made up the attacking wave – from west to east, Alexander, Franz, Elisabeth and Augusta. On their right was 1. Garde-Infanterie-Division, still under the command of the Gardekorps; on their left, the Saxons.

Surprise was total. The blow fell on the infantry of 21e and 22e Divisions d'infanterie, strung out over a front around 14km (9 miles) long. These units had been so reduced by the fighting of the previous days that all their strength was now in the front line. The Germans swept through the French positions, penetrating as far as the artillery lines. By 1200hrs they had reached the outskirts of Fère-Champenoise. Only by committing both the corps reserve and 18e Division d'infanterie, serving as the army reserve in that sector, did the French finally manage to re-form a line of defence. This finally checked the German advance, but at some 6–8km (4–5 miles) behind the original front line.

Looking north-westwards from the Signal du Poirier, the highest point on the ridge, towards the village of Saint-Prix and the crossing of the Petit Morin.

The Saxons attacked at the same time. They reached the Somme crossings with little difficulty, but had to resort to hand-to-hand fighting to capture the village of Lenharrée. Progress everywhere was slow. Further to the east, 23. Reserve-Division captured their assigned crossings, but had to clear the village of Sommesous house by house. The Saxons made it a little way south-eastwards but were held up by French artillery. And, in any case, they were exhausted. They eventually captured the heights around 4km (2 miles) to the south of the Somme and by nightfall had almost reached the line of the river Vesle, south-east of Fère-Champenoise.

For the French, the price of containing the German attack had been high. 21e Division d'infanterie had lost one brigadier, three regimental commanders and half the divisional artillery. 64e RI, facing 1. Garde-Infanterie-Division, was almost wiped out. Three battalions were reduced to just four companies – in total a little over 1,000 men of all ranks, or one-third of the regiment's strength at mobilization. In 18e Division d'infanterie, on loan from 9e Corps d'armée and not even in the front line when the attack took place, 66e RI sustained losses amounting to 25 officers and 1,287 men; 32e RI, the other regiment in the brigade, counted 15 officers and 620 men as casualties.

Alexandre Gaudon, serving with 32e RI (whose peacetime garrison was Tours), later recalled what happened as his regiment hurried to the front:

The 93e was falling back in disorder, but without much panic.... One of the first shots wounded Capitaine Baudin as the Germans approached from three sides. Four of us carried the captain as far as a hollow, where we were under fire from both sides and the rear. We had to leave him in a small pine wood, but of the four who had tried to help him, three were killed, and I was hit in the thigh.... At every moment my comrades fell, riddled with bullets. Sous-lieutenant Daras was wounded by a bullet that passed through both cheeks;

The main street of Lenharrée. In the pre-dawn attack of 8 September the village fell after a bitter struggle to elements from three regiments of the Gardekorps and XII Armeekorps

Joubert was killed by a bullet that struck his temple. We crossed about 1,500m of open ground, fired at from both sides. When we got to La Fère, they formed a company of men from several regiments. The provost gendarmes threatened with their revolvers anyone who tried to fall back further. At around midday, the artillery, east of Every, opened fire for three or four hours. We fell back to Gourgançon, but by this time, there was only around a hundred of us left from all the regiments. We bivouacked in a field between Gourgançon and Salon. The regiment lost its colonel, two battalion commanders, the captains and lieutenants of the 5th and 6th Companies, many NCOs, and about 1,000 men, either killed, wounded or missing. During the fighting, the Germans waved a white flag and held their rifles up butt first if any French came close, and then opened fire on them. They also lost a lot of men from our artillery.

The French units became hopelessly mixed as they fell back, and provisional brigades were formed with whatever units came to hand. 21e Division d'infanterie suffered badly: 41e Brigade, which should have comprised 64e RI and 65e RI, now consisted of 293e RI, plus two companies from 337e RI and two battalions from 93e RI; 42e Brigade, which was normally made up of 93e RI and 137e RI, now contained 137e RI, plus a battalion from 93e RI and a battalion from 337e RI.

Commanding 42e Brigade, Colonel Lamey reported to Foch:

[I] cannot disguise the extreme exhaustion, both physical and mental, of my men, after enduring a day of continuous fire without the opportunity to reply, nor the thirst of the men of the 137e who have been without water for 48 hours. I can hold tonight, for I do not doubt there will be night attacks; but a third such day [for the 137e had also been involved in the fighting on 7 September] will be impossible without serious repercussions, for we have only just managed to stop the men from breaking. Despite everything, you can count on us.

Lamey was killed the next day.

Général Georges Humbert (1862–1921), commander of the Division Marocaine. Foch described Humbert as 'the soul of our resistance'. The hard-fighting Division Marocaine was instrumental in saving Foch's position at Saint-Gond. Humbert's performance during the battle earned him a corps, and he ended the war in command of 3e Armée.

The Germans, however, had suffered as well. The two regiments of 64. Infanterie-Brigade had experienced heavy losses. In IR 177, casualties numbered 20 officers and 609 men, with 9 officers and 102 men reported as killed. In IR 178, total casualties amounted to 25 officers and 757 men; of these only 64 were posted as killed but another 259 were reported missing.

Meanwhile on the right Bülow made little effort. He had been counting on III and IX Armeekorps to guard his right flank. But Kluck had recalled both corps the previous night. Committing his last reserve – 13. Infanterie-Division – to bolster that sector, Bülow felt his only option was to go on the defensive, pulling back the whole of his right wing behind the Petit Morin. Following up, the French first retook Soizy-aux-Bois and then Saint-Prix. Supported by 10e Corps d'armée, the Division Marocaine and 42e Division d'infanterie managed to clear most of the southern bank of the Petit Morin by 0900hrs. But in the face of heavy fire they found it impossible to cross the river.

At the eastern end of the marshes, 14. Infanterie-Division – the other half of VII Armeekorps – was now committed at the shoulder of the advancing Gardekorps. On hearing of the attack, General Emmich, commanding X Armeekorps, insisted that he too should join in at their western end. His counterattack, launched by 20. Infanterie-Division, regained Saint-Prix, moved left to recapture the spur of the Crête du Poirier, and then left again to the Oyes–Mondement area. The attacks fell on the two wings of the, by now thinly extended, Division Marocaine, already in difficulty following the retreat of 11e Corps d'armée from the Somme. The Moroccans were forced to pull back southwards to higher ground, leaving the routes across the marshes free.

9e Armée was now under extreme pressure. In the centre it had lost control of the crossings over the marshes. On the right its link with 4e Armée had been compromised. And the situation of 11e Corps d'armée was very shaky indeed. But Foch knew he was not the only one in trouble. With 5e Armée advancing on the French left, Bülow was experiencing difficulties of his own.

Back at 9e Armée HQ Foch sensed a slight slackening of pressure on his left, as Bülow's right flank withdrew north of the Petit Morin. At 0700hrs he telephoned Général Langle de Cary, commanding 4e Armée. Could 21e Corps d'armée mount an attack on the German flank to bring some relief to his right? But 4e Armée could do nothing to help. Under attack by 3. and 4. Armeen around Vitry-le-François, Langle de Cary was down to his last reserves. Foch then turned to Franchet d'Esperey. Was 5e Armée in a position to attack and disengage the left of 9e Corps d'armée? This time the response was positive. At 0730hrs Franchet d'Esperey undertook to swing 10e Corps d'armée around to face northwards and then north-eastwards.

Despite his perilous situation, Foch's instincts were still to attack. 11e Corps d'armée was ordered to retake Fère-Champenoise; the 9e Division de cavalerie was to demonstrate on the French right, towards Sommesous. But, that evening, as further reports came in from his battered regiments, Foch realized that more was needed to secure his positions. At 2120hrs he turned again to 5e Armée. Could 10e Corps d'armée perhaps extend its front, so allowing him to withdraw 42e Division d'infanterie for use as a mobile reserve? Once again Franchet d'Esperey agreed, and very generously released 10e Corps d'armée to Foch's command. Foch was at last able to withdraw the shattered 42e Division d'infanterie from the line. Then by redistributing his command he managed to stabilize his front. The positions of 9e Corps

TOP
Looking south from
Mondement towards Oyes.
The Germans advanced
alongside the road just
visible on the right.

BOTTOM
The château at Mondement
today. Reduced to a burnt-out
shell by the fighting, it was
rebuilt in its original style.

d'armée rested around Mondement, while 11e Corps d'armée withdrew beyond La Fère-Champenoise. Foch contacted Joffre with a famously laconic (and quite possibly apocryphal) situation report: 'Strong pressure on my right; my centre giving way; impossible to move; situation excellent; I am attacking.'

9 September

Yet the following day it was not Foch who attacked, but Bülow and Hausen. The key position now became the village and château of Mondement, commanding the northern approach to the Allemant Ridge. If the Germans succeeded in breaking through here, the way lay open to the Seine. From a small rise, both village and chateau looked northwards over the Saint-Gond marshes. This was where the Germans were advancing, making the location ideal both as an observation post and as an artillery position. Foch's orders for the day therefore emphasized the importance of retaining the high ground between La Villeneuve-lès-Charleville and Mondement.

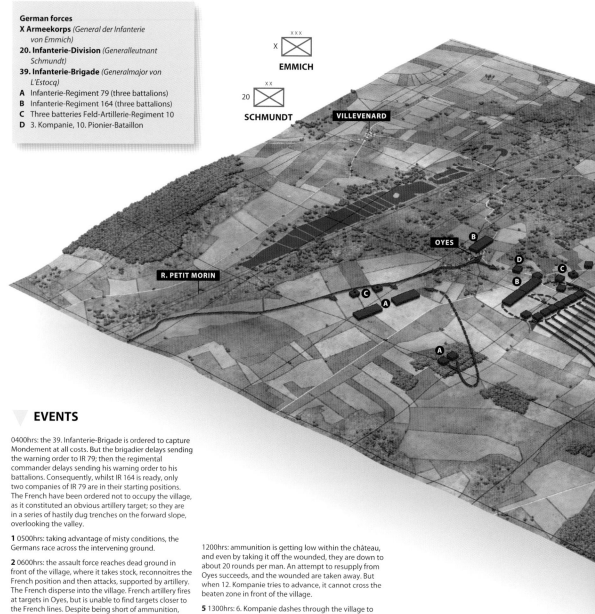

German forces

X Armeekorps *(General der Infanterie von Emmich)*

20. Infanterie-Division *(Generalleutnant Schmundt)*

39. Infanterie-Brigade *(Generalmajor von L'Estocq)*

A Infanterie-Regiment 79 (three battalions)
B Infanterie-Regiment 164 (three battalions)
C Three batteries Feld-Artillerie-Regiment 10
D 3. Kompanie, 10. Pionier-Bataillon

XXX
X EMMICH

XX
20 SCHMUNDT

VILLEVENARD

OYES

R. PETIT MORIN

▼ EVENTS

0400hrs: the 39. Infanterie-Brigade is ordered to capture Mondement at all costs. But the brigadier delays sending the warning order to IR 79; then the regimental commander delays sending his warning order to his battalions. Consequently, whilst IR 164 is ready, only two companies of IR 79 are in their starting positions. The French have been ordered not to occupy the village, as it constituted an obvious artillery target; so they are in a series of hastily dug trenches on the forward slope, overlooking the valley.

1 0500hrs: taking advantage of misty conditions, the Germans race across the intervening ground.

2 0600hrs: the assault force reaches dead ground in front of the village, where it takes stock, reconnoitres the French position and then attacks, supported by artillery. The French disperse into the village. French artillery fires at targets in Oyes, but is unable to find targets closer to the French lines. Despite being short of ammunition, the Germans succeed in winkling the French out of each house and farm, until a small group seizes the château about 0915hrs. The French, already under strength, disperse into the woods. A party from a neighbouring battalion attempts to capture the château, but is driven off.

3 1000hrs: the château is held by about 130 Germans, mostly from I./IR 164. The companies of II./IR 164 remain north of the village church, pinned in the open by French artillery, which is now beginning to get its bearings. 9. Kompanie tries to cross the open ground from Oyes as reinforcements, but is halted by artillery fire.

4 1100hrs: the French counterattack from the south-east. Only two weak companies strong, they are easily driven off.

1200hrs: ammunition is getting low within the château, and even by taking it off the wounded, they are down to about 20 rounds per man. An attempt to resupply from Oyes succeeds, and the wounded are taken away. But when 12. Kompanie tries to advance, it cannot cross the beaten zone in front of the village.

5 1300hrs: 6. Kompanie dashes through the village to join the defenders in the château. Soon afterwards, French reinforcements arrive in the form of 77e RI. They attack immediately, and after hand-to-hand fighting in the château gardens, are driven off with heavy losses.

6 1400hrs: the 77e mount another attack, equally unsuccessful and equally costly.

7 1500hrs: two officers and a number of gunners of 49e RA manhandle two pieces through the woods to fire directly on the château; at the same time German artillery rounds start falling short. The upper floors of the château are abandoned because of the artillery fire.

1800hrs: the Germans decide to abandon the château and withdraw, taking all their wounded with them.

1830hrs: the French mount another attack, but the Germans are no longer there.

THE STRUGGLE FOR MONDEMENT, 9 SEPTEMBER 1914

The French hold this crucial ridge as the Germans attempt an audacious breakthrough.

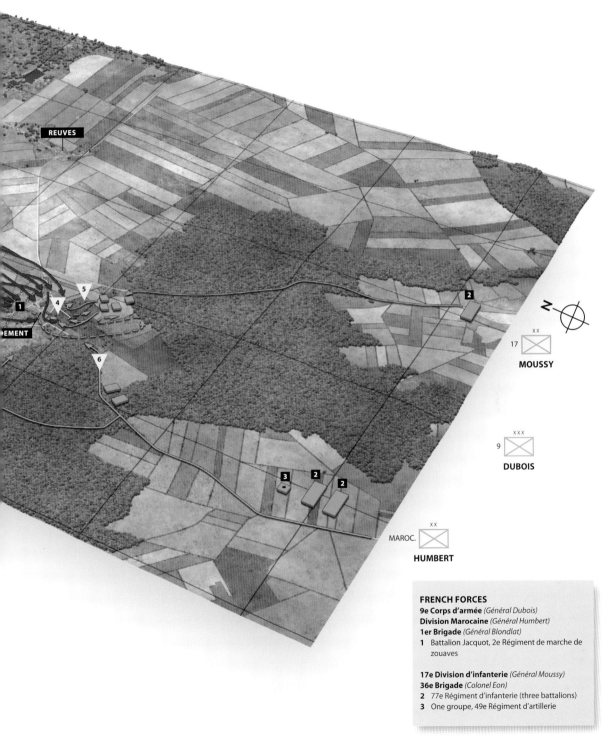

REUVES

EMENT

5

1

4

6

2

MOUSSY
17 ☒☒

9 ☒☒☒
DUBOIS

3   2   2

MAROC. ☒☒
HUMBERT

FRENCH FORCES
9e Corps d'armée (Général Dubois)
Division Marocaine (Général Humbert)
1er Brigade (Général Blondlat)
1 Battalion Jacquot, 2e Régiment de marche de zouaves

17e Division d'infanterie (Général Moussy)
36e Brigade (Colonel Eon)
2 77e Régiment d'infanterie (three battalions)
3 One groupe, 49e Régiment d'artillerie

Another view of the château at Mondement, this time from the west. On the right is one of the breaches in the wall of the kitchen garden. 77e RI tried to use these to attack the château. But the breaches were narrow and the German fire accurate.

Responsibility for holding Mondement fell to the RM du 2e Zouaves, supported by two batteries of 49e RA. But following a number of misunderstandings and mistakes the village fell to a *coup de main* by the Hanoverians of IR 164. An immediate counterattack by the 2e failed. But reinforcements from 77e RI were drafted in and Mondement was eventually retaken after a struggle that lasted all afternoon.

On the left 10e Corps d'armée went on the attack again. By 1100hrs 20e Division d'infanterie had forced the passage of the Petit Morin and started to climb the steep northern slopes of the valley. The 20e then turned eastwards and slowly drove the enemy from its positions. By late evening 51e Division de réserve had retaken Saint-Prix, and the Germans were continuing to fall back. The pressure exerted in this sector forced them to recall units from the Mondement area. And all had to retreat back to the north side of the marshes.

In Kirchbach's battlegroup, on the German left, Hausen replaced 2. Garde-Infanterie-Division with 24. Reserve-Division, newly released after the fall of Givet. Restored once more to two-division strength, the Gardekorps continued its attacks. In another dawn assault, observed by a French officer, the Garde caught and dispersed the French counterattack just as it was forming. The German troops 'advanced in perfect order by platoons in line abreast, separated by wide intervals, with other groups behind in checker-board pattern, followed by others in one or two ranks. Behind each group were officers, sword in one hand, revolver in the other, encouraging their men forward with loud cries. The whole lot marched with a firm, regular pace, giving a real impression of power and resolution.'

Pressing on south-westwards, the Gardekorps captured the village of Connantre after heavy fighting. A pause was called just after midday.

TOP

The north-facing wall of the château at Mondement. While the men of IR 164 tried to defend the building, French and German shelling had set the roof alight and rendered many of the rooms untenable.

BOTTOM

The marshes of Saint-Gond, after winter rain in 1914. This shows the inherent nature of the ground and thus the importance of dominating the causeways that carried the roads.

Exhausted, the men dropped where they stood and fell asleep. In the afternoon, as they approached Fère-Champenoise, the corps commander, General der Infanterie Freiherr von Plettenberg, ordered them to attack again. The 2. G.R.z.Fß were briefly distracted by the discovery of a store of large cheeses. But the French artillery also ensured that little progress was made that afternoon.

Hausen tried to support the Garde with a three-division attack, involving 24. Reserve-Division, 32. Infanterie-Division and 23. Reserve-Division. But faulty staff work sent the 24. attacking across the front of 2. Garde-Infanterie-Division, and the resulting confusion slowed down the whole operation. By nightfall, however, the Saxons had reached the line of the Maurienne. And the Garde was only a few kilometres away from rolling up the whole French line.

THE GARDE AT FÈRE-CHAMPENOISE, 9 SEPTEMBER (pp. 60–61)

During the opening actions of the war, the regimental colour remained essential on campaign for both the French and the Germans. The British had already learnt in 1881 that the colour bearer became an immediate target, resulting in unnecessary casualties. But a captured colour was an immediate propaganda success for the enemy, so its protection remained an paramount. When the Garde (**1**) attacked at La Fère-Champenoise, on 9 September, Fahnenjunker Unteroffizier Freiherr von der Recke von der Horst of the Füsilier Battalion, Alexander Grenadiers was killed almost immediately; his place was taken by Füsilier Samuelson, who was likewise killed, just ten minutes later. After a final colour bearer was killed, the colour (**2**) lay on the ground un-noticed in the confusion of the battle; fortunately, it was later rescued by a soldier from another regiment. The Germans lost three colours during the battle – those of II./IR 66 near Betz on 6th September, I./Füs.R. 36, at Vincy on the 7th, and II./RIR 94 near Senlis on the 10th. A fourth, that of II./IR 27, was buried to prevent its capture on the 10th; it was recovered by French troops on 4 October. The French lost no regimental colours, although some tricolours were found by men of IR 77 in the baggage of a regiment of *zouaves* near Courjonnet on 6 September. They may have been company markers or patriotic gifts to the troops – they were certainly not regimental colours in the strict sense. The three German colours, together with three others captured during 1914, were paraded through the streets of Paris and ceremonially handed over to the Governor of the Invalides, to install them with other French trophies in the chapel there. Colours would have no place in trench warfare: orders were given to return German colours to their regimental depots on 12 July 1915; the French retained theirs in the field, but generally kept safely at regimental headquarters.

Foch, meanwhile, was still trying to create a reserve from his battered divisions. The only formation available to him was 42e Division d'infanterie – so recently withdrawn from the line – and its thinned ranks were moved into position on the right, behind 11e Corps d'armée. Foch planned to launch a counterattack at 1715hrs. Seven divisions from 9e and 11e Corps d'armée would take part – their objective to drive the Germans back to the Somme. But the exhausted 42e did not reach its start line until nightfall and the attack was postponed.

10 September

The planned offensive eventually began before dawn, but it fell largely on air. At 1045hrs the previous morning, and unbeknown to Foch, Bülow had taken the decision to retreat. Without reserves, he was unable to restore the situation on his right, where Franchet d'Esperey and his men were continuing to push into the gap between 2. and 1. Armeen. Bülow's response was to withdraw 2. Armee to the north bank of the Marne. To confuse the French, he ordered that all current attacks should continue. But, by 1600hrs, the divisional baggage trains had started on their way. Then, an hour later, the infantry began to move northwards, leaving strong rearguards behind.

But Bülow neglected to inform 3. Armee of his decision until the afternoon. And, with the retreat well under way, OHL told Hausen to support a new attack by 4. Armee. So Hausen was ordering his men to advance on the left, while his neighbour was retreating on the right. Hausen's right wing had to pull back to conform with 2. Armee's withdrawal. His daring plan had failed.

On the morning of 10 September, 10e Corps d'armée – by now aligned almost north–south – pushed forwards, hoping to roll up the German line. Stout defence by the German rearguards slowed their advance considerably, but still they made significant progress. This allowed 9e Corps d'armée to wheel eastwards and join 11e Corps d'armée in putting their full weight into opposing the Gardekorps. By evening elements of both had reached the line of the Somme once more.

Foch issued orders to pursue the Germans. But his men were exhausted and the weather had broken. In the event, 9e Armée could do little more than follow the enemy, trying to turn the German rearguards from their positions.

The battle of Saint-Gond was fought over terrain that favoured the defence. The marshes served to canalize the German advance along predictable lines, restricting the amount of force the enemy could bring to bear on any given point. The ambiguous role allotted to 3. Armee also did much to hamper the invading force. Pulled between requests to support his two neighbours, Hausen was never allowed to concentrate his forces to best effect. Illness too played its part. Dysentery had struck Hausen in the course of the campaign, undoubtedly affecting his performance. And ill health may also have afflicted Bülow, with suggestions that he suffered a small stroke during the opening days of the battle.

On the French side, Foch was certainly helped by the unselfish cooperation of Franchet d'Esperey in releasing 10e Corps d'armée at a critical juncture. But the victory at Saint-Gond belonged to Foch alone. The attack of the Gardekorps and the near-collapse of 11e Corps d'armée left the French on the brink of defeat. But, as Foch himself remarked, 'A battle is lost only if you believe it to be lost.'

The battle of the two Morins, 6–9 September 1914

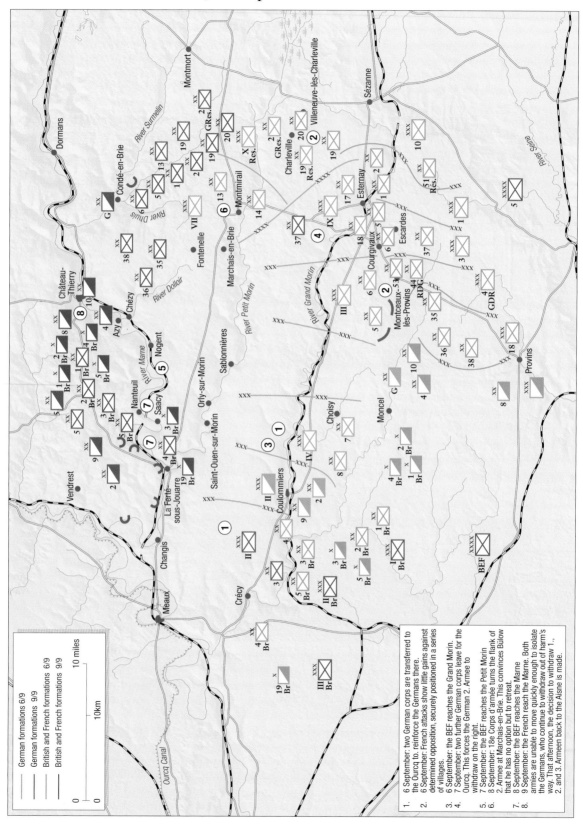

1. 6 September: two German corps are transferred to the Ourcq to. reinforce the Germans there.
2. 6 September: French attacks show little gains against determined opposition, securely positioned in a series of villages.
3. 6 September: the BEF reaches the Grand Morin.
4. 7 September: two further German corps leave for the Ourcq. This forces the German 2. Armee to withdraw on the right.
5. 7 September: the BEF reaches the Petit Morin
6. 8 September: 18e Corps d'armée turns the flank of 2. Armee at Marchais-en-Brie. This convinces Bülow that he has no option but to retreat.
7. 8 September: the BEF reaches the Marne
8. 9 September: the French reach the Marne. Both armies are unable to move quickly enough to isolate the Germans, who continue to withdraw out of harm's way. That afternoon, the decision to withdraw 1., 2. and 3. Armeen back to the Aisne is made.

THE BATTLE OF THE TWO MORINS, 6–11 SEPTEMBER

After checking the German advance at Guise on 29 August, 5e Armée had used the opportunity to slip away southwards. But Lanrezac was increasingly pessimistic about the chances of stopping the German onslaught – and more particularly about Joffre's ability to do so. Nor did he mind voicing his opinions. Such public criticism of a superior could never be tolerated and Joffre was certainly not prepared to do so. On 3 September he sacked Lanrezac and replaced him with Franchet d'Esperey, the commander of 1er Corps.

As it fell back, 5e Armée was becoming increasingly stretched in trying to stay in contact with the BEF on the left and 9e Armée on the right. Priority was given to maintaining a continuous front on the right. So Général Conneau's Corps de cavalerie was thrust into the resulting gap on the left – between 18e Corps d'armée and the BEF – a gap 1. Armee was poised to enter.

On 4 September Franchet d'Esperey met with Sir Henry Wilson, Deputy Chief of Staff to Sir John French, at Bray-sur-Seine. The two men agreed a plan of action for resuming the offensive on 6 September. The BEF was to turn back north, extend to the left to link up with 6e Armée on the Ourcq – taking up position on a line between Changis and Coulommiers – and then attack eastwards towards Montmirail. 5e Armée would also have Montmirail as its objective, attacking from the south.

At 0915hrs on 5 September Franchet d'Esperey received bad news. The British would not be able to attack as planned. They had continued their retreat overnight and would be unable to reach the start line in time. British participation was vital to the offensive and Joffre went in person to BEF headquarters to see Sir John French. Joffre was eventually reduced to banging the table to drive home his point: 'The honour of England is at stake.' But his intervention had the desired effect. Sir John turned bright red and promised his full cooperation in the counterattack.

5e Armée slowly put a halt to its rearward movements and took up its positions. The men were all very tired and some units had taken heavy casualties in the previous month. 18e RI had lost 1,000 men since the outbreak of war, 600 of those at Guise. Even the bullish Franchet d'Esperey was not completely confident of the outcome: 'My army can fight on the 6th but [it] is not in a brilliant situation; the three reserve divisions cannot be counted on.' He was a little more forthright with his artillery commander: 'I'm sick of this f***ing retreating; we're attacking.' And attack they did, led by their energetic commander.

By his willingness to move on to the offensive, Franchet d'Esperey opened the way to victory, for it was his 5e Armée that would strike at the enemy. Joffre was fully aware of Franchet d'Esperey's importance: '[His] role… on September 4th, 1914,' he later wrote, 'merits being underlined in history: it is he who made possible the battle of the Marne.'

6 September

French aerial reconnaissance had noted the movements of a large body of troops away from 5e Armée's front. These were the units from Kluck's II and IV Armeekorps, recalled to the Ourcq to face Maunoury's men. And the gap they left gave the Allies their opportunity. Franchet d'Esperey issued his orders accordingly: 18e Corps d'armée (Maud'huy) was to attack towards Montceaux-lès-Provins, 3e Corps d'armée (Hache) towards Courgivaux, and

Général Franchet d'Esperey, commander of the French Fifth Army. 'I'm tired of this f***ing retreating,' Franchet d'Esperey told his artillery commander. 'we're attacking.'

Général Louis de Maud'huy (1857–1921) commander of 18e Corps d'armée. Maud'huy rose to command an army for a short period in 1915, but most of his commands were at corps level. He ended the war as an inspector of training battalions.

1er Corps d'armée (Deligny) towards Esternay. Finally 10e Corps d'armée was to do what it could to support 1er Corps d'armée on its left, while also keeping in touch with 9e Armée on its other flank. The Corps de cavalerie (Conneau) was to play a dual role – on its right supporting 18e Corps d'armée, and on its left covering the flank of the BEF.

The fighting took place over the Brie Plateau – that rolling, cultivated plain cut through by the deep valleys of the Marne, Grand Morin and Petit Morin. The rivers were slow flowing but unfordable, and could be crossed only at a small number of bridging points. The valleys themselves were heavily wooded, with more woods – large and small – dotted over the countryside. The hills on the northern banks of the rivers were generally higher than those on the south.

It was afternoon before the French finally made contact with the Germans. The commander of 18e Corps d'armée, Général Maud'huy, was a firm believer in the power of artillery and directed massive firepower against Montceaux-lès-Provins. Firing three to four rounds a minute, the whole of his corps, divisional and reserve group artillery – some 200 guns in all – was brought to bear against the village. The German guns were soon silenced under the weight of the barrage. Then the French artillery turned its attention to individual farmhouses. The Germans were winkled out of these one by one (but only at considerable cost – one farmhouse alone cost 6e Division d'infanterie 600 men). It was not until 2300hrs that the village was finally secured.

Elsewhere progress was just as slow. The small town of Esternay proved a real obstacle. IX Armeekorps retaining control despite a direct assault and flanking moves from both north and south. Meanwhile the Corps de cavalerie was playing little part in the attack, their posture characterized by one French history as 'cautiously defensive'. It made no aggressive moves. But nor did it unsaddle, feed or water the horses! On the far right 10e Corps d'armée formed the pivot around which 5e Armée would swing. It met with more success – capturing the village of Charleville, overlooking the valley of the Petit Morin.

By evening the BEF had reached the line Crécy–Coulommiers–Choisy. Indeed, II and III Corps had got as far as the banks of the Grand Morin. Clashes had occurred between the British cavalry, acting as advanced guards, and some German detachments. But the enemy had been brushed aside with little difficulty.

Aerial reconnaissance continued to reveal extensive German troop movements behind the lines: IV Armeekorps was still moving northwards. That evening, with his flank left exposed by the withdrawal of IV Armeekorps, Bülow decided that he had to bolster his defences. III and IX Armeekorps were still on loan from 1. Armee. They would fall back to the north bank of the Petit Morin, west of Montmirail, with III Armeekorps acting as flank guard. But later that night Kluck asked for his troops back and Bülow's plan came to nothing. When Kluck's order came through, both corps were under attack – III Armeekorps from 18e Corps d'armée and IX Armeekorps from 3e Corps d'armée – and they had to disengage from action before they could begin to move.

By transferring these men to the battle of the Ourcq, Kluck increased the gap between 1. and 2. Armeen, and there were few troops left to fill it. Bülow's right flank position was now held by VII Armeekorps (Einem), already short of one division, which had been sent to plug a gap on the left. Bülow was forced to turn to 3. Armee for help. Meanwhile he sent two divisions of Richthofen's Höherer Kavallerie-Kommandeur 1 to provide cover.

7 September

Franchet d'Esperey was insistent that his forces maintain a solid line as they advanced, and framed his orders accordingly. All formations were to make sure they kept in contact with their neighbours. On the left the Corps de cavalerie and 18e Corps d'armée were to align themselves with the BEF, while on the right 1er Corps d'armée was to align with 10e Corps d'armée – effectively restricting the centre to the speed of the flanks. Early that morning all the evidence indicated that the Germans opposite 5e Armée were in full retreat. The way seemed clear for an advance, with the town of Montmirail as the objective for the day.

Conneau's Corps de cavalerie advanced as far as the river Aubentin, but it was held up there by German rearguards. His horses had been so debilitated by the campaign so far that he was unable to send out strategic reconnaissance patrols and all the units stuck close to one another.

To their right 18e Corps d'armée advanced to the Grand Morin without a fight. Maud'huy ordered his men to pursue the Germans as far as the Petit Morin. But by nightfall only a few units had managed to cross the Grand Morin. At daybreak 3e Corps d'armée was also on the Grand Morin. Here a fragment of IX Armeekorps, as yet unaware of the order to retreat, attacked. The French picket line was driven in. But the two divisions, commanded in contrasting style by the tigerish Mangin (5e Division d'infanterie) and the more careful Pétain (6e Division d'infanterie), captured Escardes and Courgivaux and pushed the Germans back across the Grand Morin. Meanwhile 1er Corps continued its attack on Esternay. But it was soon apparent that the Germans had already evacuated the town and it was occupied without opposition. 1er Corps d'armée and elements from 10e Corps d'armée then prepared to pursue the fleeing enemy: the immediate objective, Montmirail.

That evening, however, came news came of the difficulties facing 9e Armée. Soizy-aux-Bois was lost and Sézanne – whose capture would split 9e Armée from the 5e – was under threat. 10e Corps d'armée was immediately ordered to stop pursuing the Germans. It was time now to turn eastwards instead, mounting an attack to relieve the pressure falling on the 9e.

Meanwhile, the BEF continued their careful advance. Near the village of Moncel a troop of 9th Lancers, accompanied by a machine gun, boldly took on a squadron of G.Drag.R. 1. A second squadron from the same German regiment was also repulsed with heavy losses by a squadron of 18th Hussars, fighting dismounted.

8 September

Believing that Bülow would fight for the line of the Petit Morin, Franchet d'Esperey urged his commanders to press the retreating Germans closely and give them no time to form a defensive line. Messages from the Ourcq were still optimistic. According to 6e Armée, it had pushed the enemy back and there were no Germans in front of the BEF. Aerial reconnaissance backed this up: large German columns were crossing the Marne at La Ferté-sous-Jouarre and Château-Thierry. But the news was not all positive. Foch still urgently needed support and this would divert manpower from Franchet d'Esperey's own attacks.

By evening the British were just short of the Petit Morin, where they found the going somewhat problematic. The Petit Morin itself was a slow-moving stream, some 6m (20ft) wide. But it ran through a steep, wooded valley,

THE ATTACK ON MONTCEAUX-LÈS-PROVINS, 6 SEPTEMBER (pp. 68–69)

The conventional wisdom of the pre-war French Army was that prolonged bombardments were a waste of shells. However, the village of Montceaux-lès-Provins was defended by the three battalions of IR 20, supported by four batteries of Felda.R. 39, with elements of Füs.R. 39 and IR 24 in reserve, and would have been impossible to capture without prolonged artillery support. The bombardment, which involved the combined artillery of Pétain's 6e Division d'infanterie as well as that of 18e Corps, began at 0600hrs; one hour later, the artillery of 53e and 69e Divisions de réserve joined in. One German artilleryman described the French fire as 'monstrous.… Everything was covered in columns of black smoke, so high and broad that I could hardly see anything; in between were white shrapnel bursts. Limbers and riderless horses emerged from time to time fleeing Montceaux.' Through a long morning and afternoon, the village and its surroundings were pounded. Eventually, at around 1700hrs, the men of 123e RI, supported on either flank by those of the 6e and 119e, were able to capture the burning ruins with little difficulty. There are no German casualty figures for this action – however, during the whole battle, IR 20 lost 3 officers and 121 men killed, and 53 officers and 2,074 men wounded. Felda.R. 39 appears to have got off relatively lightly, losing only one officer and 12 men killed during the whole of the battle; the number of wounded is not known. French casualties too remain unknown – the war diary of the 123e makes no mention of casualties at all. Although an infantryman, Pétain was convinced of the value of artillery support, only committing his men after a thorough preparation, even if it made him appear out of step with the rest of the Army. It was here that he supposedly uttered his famous dictum, 'artillery conquers: infantry occupies'.

This plate shows the French 75s (**1**) with their four-man crews (**2**). To the rear stands the officer (**3**) commanding the battery.

bordered on both sides by close country with a large number of copses, villages and hamlets. More importantly, there were only six places where the river could be crossed. The town of Montmirail was deemed a key position. Occupying a high spur, it dominated the valley, with views both east and west.

The first attempts by the BEF to seize a bridge intact were all rebuffed. 5th Dragoon Guards attempted to rush the bridge at Sablonnières, while 4th Dragoon Guards attempted to do the same at La Forge. The Royal Scots Greys caught a party of German infantry having breakfast at Gibraltar, near Saint-Ouen-sur-Morin. A few shells scattered them, but German artillery prevented the British from exploiting the ensuing confusion. A final attempt by 5th Lancers at Orly-sur-Morin was also driven off by well-placed artillery. By 0830hrs the advance had seemingly stalled.

Only the arrival of the infantry made further movement possible. With the aid of dismounted British cavalry and mounted French troopers, 1st Black Watch and 1st Cameron Highlanders prised open the defences around Sablonnières. By 1300hrs they had captured the crossing intact. To the west 1st Duke of Cornwall's Light Infantry and 1st East Surrey Regiment made further crossings in the teeth of determined opposition. These successes forced the remaining Germans to withdraw to prevent encirclement. By late afternoon the British had forced the Germans back to the south bank of the Marne at La Ferté-sous-Jouarre, but a violent thunderstorm at 1800hrs brought the day's operations to a close.

On the right 10e Corps d'armée was turning eastwards to join Foch's battle. So 1er Corps d'armée had to slide in the same direction to keep in touch. Its progress over the plateau to the south of Montmirail was slowed considerably by indirect German fire. Aerial reconnaissance could not spot the enemy guns and the French were unable to neutralize them. French artillery responded by covering likely positions with a barrage. This seemed to work and German fire slackened. Advancing once more, 1er Corps d'armée succeeded in forcing crossings of the Petit Morin, to the east of Montmirail.

1er Corps d'armée was now moving right, 3e Corps d'armée had to follow. Mangin's 5e Division d'infanterie took the lead but could move only slowly across the approaches to Montmirail. German artillery covered the exit to every village and the shelling was incessant. It took most of the day to cover the 7km (4 miles) needed to reach the south bank of the Petit Morin. At 2000hrs Mangin tried to rush the crossings. But his men were driven back by artillery and he postponed the attack until the following morning.

The bridge over the Petit Morin at La Ferté-sous-Jouarre. The retreating British had blown up the bridge. Two field companies of Royal Engineers, the 23rd and 26th, were responsible for destroying four bridges in this sector. But they lacked the time to do the job thoroughly and IV Armeekorps was able to cross here.

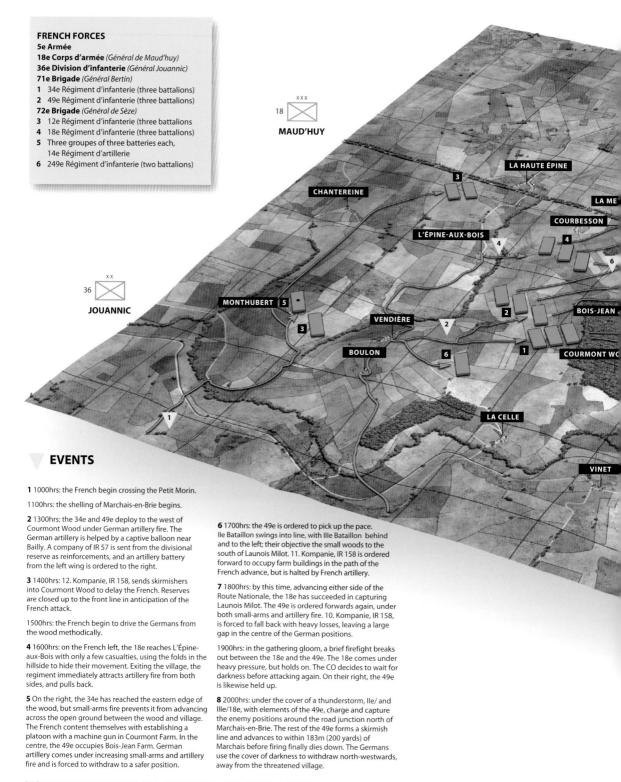

▼ EVENTS

1 1000hrs: the French begin crossing the Petit Morin.

1100hrs: the shelling of Marchais-en-Brie begins.

2 1300hrs: the 34e and 49e deploy to the west of Courmont Wood under German artillery fire. The German artillery is helped by a captive balloon near Bailly. A company of IR 57 is sent from the divisional reserve as reinforcements, and an artillery battery from the left wing is ordered to the right.

3 1400hrs: 12. Kompanie, IR 158, sends skirmishers into Courmont Wood to delay the French. Reserves are closed up to the front line in anticipation of the French attack.

1500hrs: the French begin to drive the Germans from the wood methodically.

4 1600hrs: on the French left, the 18e reaches L'Épine-aux-Bois with only a few casualties, using the folds in the hillside to hide their movement. Exiting the village, the regiment immediately attracts artillery fire from both sides, and pulls back.

5 On the right, the 34e has reached the eastern edge of the wood, but small-arms fire prevents it from advancing across the open ground between the wood and village. The French content themselves with establishing a platoon with a machine gun in Courmont Farm. In the centre, the 49e occupies Bois-Jean Farm. German artillery comes under increasing small-arms and artillery fire and is forced to withdraw to a safer position.

6 1700hrs: the 49e is ordered to pick up the pace. IIe Bataillon swings into line, with IIIe Bataillon behind and to the left; their objective the small woods to the south of Launois Milot. 11. Kompanie, IR 158 is ordered forward to occupy farm buildings in the path of the French advance, but is halted by French artillery.

7 1800hrs: by this time, advancing either side of the Route Nationale, the 18e has succeeded in capturing Launois Milot. The 49e is ordered forwards again, under both small-arms and artillery fire. 10. Kompanie, IR 158, is forced to fall back with heavy losses, leaving a large gap in the centre of the German positions.

1900hrs: in the gathering gloom, a brief firefight breaks out between the 18e and the 49e. The 18e comes under heavy pressure, but holds on. The CO decides to wait for darkness before attacking again. On their right, the 49e is likewise held up.

8 2000hrs: under the cover of a thunderstorm, IIe/ and IIIe/18e, with elements of the 49e, charge and capture the enemy positions around the road junction north of Marchais-en-Brie. The rest of the 49e forms a skirmish line and advances to within 183m (200 yards) of Marchais before firing finally dies down. The Germans use the cover of darkness to withdraw north-westwards, away from the threatened village.

TURNING THE GERMAN FLANK – MARCHAIS-EN-BRIE, 8 SEPTEMBER 1914

The French succeed in finding the open flank of the German 2. Armee in the decisive encounter of the whole ba

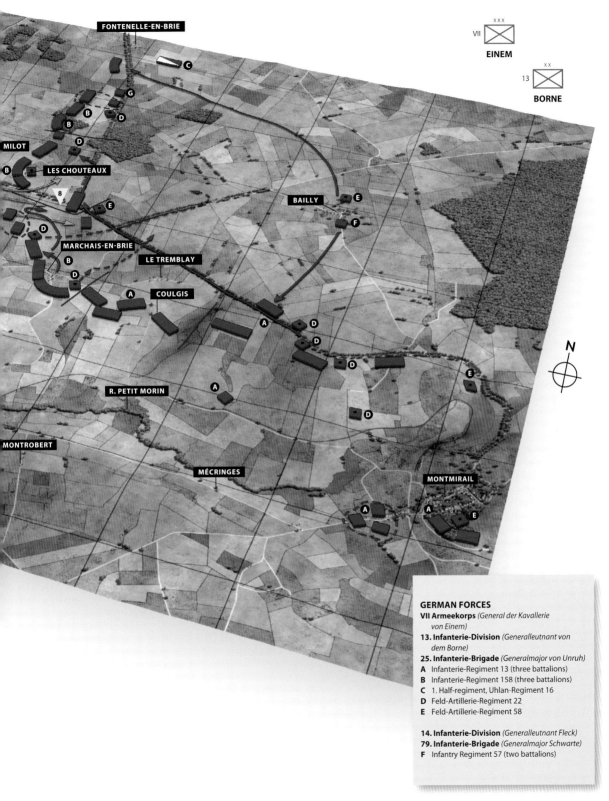

FONTENELLE-EN-BRIE

MILOT

LES CHOUTEAUX

MARCHAIS-EN-BRIE

LE TREMBLAY

COULGIS

BAILLY

R. PETIT MORIN

MONTROBERT

MÉCRINGES

MONTMIRAIL

VII ⊠ xxx
EINEM

13 ⊠ xx
BORNE

GERMAN FORCES
VII Armeekorps *(General der Kavallerie von Einem)*
13. Infanterie-Division *(Generalleutnant von dem Borne)*
25. Infanterie-Brigade *(Generalmajor von Unruh)*
A   Infanterie-Regiment 13 (three battalions)
B   Infanterie-Regiment 158 (three battalions)
C   1. Half-regiment, Uhlan-Regiment 16
D   Feld-Artillerie-Regiment 22
E   Feld-Artillerie-Regiment 58

14. Infanterie-Division *(Generalleutnant Fleck)*
79. Infanterie-Brigade *(Generalmajor Schwarte)*
F   Infantry Regiment 57 (two battalions)

TOP

Montmirail seen from the west. The town looks out in both directions along the valley of the Petit Morin. The Germans held the ridgeline on the left of the picture. The river lies behind the trees on the right.

BOTTOM

Looking westwards from Marchais-en-Brie. Most of the trees in the foreground did not exist in 1914. From this point the Germans were able to dominate the exits from the distant wood for much of the action and so prevent the French from advancing.

It was left to 18e Corps d'armée to strike the decisive blow. At Marchais-en-Brie it found the right flank of Bülow's 2. Armee, left in the air by 1. Armee's withdrawal. 19. Infanterie-Division held Montmirail and its eastern approaches, but, to the west of the town, the spur of Marchais-en-Brie was occupied by 13. Infanterie-Division, with its flank refused as far as Fontenelle. Side by side, 35e and 36e Divisions d'infanterie reached the Petit Morin by 1030hrs and the advanced guards crossed without any difficulty. Throughout the afternoon 35e Division d'infanterie forced the Germans from one position to another. Then a final night-time attack definitively drove the Germans out of the village.

With Marchais in French hands, Montmirail was untenable. And, if Montmirail was untenable, the whole of 2. Armee was now in difficulties. That evening Franchet d'Esperey issued a message to his men: 'The enemy is in full retreat. There must be no stopping for enemy rearguards that will try and sacrifice themselves to slow us down. They must be wiped out by artillery

fire, turned by the infantry and pursued by the cavalry. Only a vigorous pursuit will enable us to reap the rewards of the situation.'

The historic significance of a victory on the old Napoleonic battlefield of Montmirail, where Napoleon had defeated Blücher's Prussians in 1814, was not lost on Franchet d'Esperey. But there was no time to linger. The Corps de cavalerie was sent with the BEF, 18e Corps d'armée towards Château-Thierry, and 1er Corps d'armée and the reserve divisions northwards towards Condé-en-Brie. 10e Corps d'armée was to move forwards, ready to go either north or east depending on the situation. The bridging trains were also ordered forwards, Franchet d'Esperey believing – quite rightly – that many of the Marne bridges had been blown up during the Allied retreat.

In the event 10e Corps d'armée went east. When Foch got in touch that evening, asking for support to help disengage 42e Division d'infanterie, Franchet d'Esperey did not hesitate. He immediately put the 10e at Foch's disposal.

Always a cautious commander, Bülow was by now extremely concerned. At 0400hrs he had contacted OHL. Casualties had reduced his army to the equivalent of three corps; nevertheless, he would still continue to attack. Four hours later came even more disquieting news – this time from Richthofen's Höherer Kavallerie-Kommandeur 1. The German front had been breached and Richthofen was pulling his divisions back to the line of the river Dolloir, which flowed into the Marne at Chézy. A 30km (19-mile) gap, devoid of German troops, now existed between Montmirail and the Marne. This prompted a flurry of activity at OHL, and the head of intelligence, Oberstleutnant Hentsch, was sent to the front once more.

In choosing Hentsch, Moltke was confiding the mission to a trusted subordinate. Uncertain communications between OHL and the armies – broken telephone lines, inefficient radios – had left Moltke fearing he was missing information vital to the conduct of the campaign. But he also felt that the personal touch was best: 'commanding generals must be informed about the intentions of the High Command, but this is best accomplished orally by sending an officer from headquarters.' Hentsch's mission was to

LEFT
General Sir Douglas Haig, commander of I Corps. Haig succeeded French as commander of the BEF, but his reputation remains controversial to this day.

CENTRE
General Sir Horace Smith-Dorrien, commander of II Corps. In his report on the battle of Le Cateau, Sir John French put aside their mutual antagonism to refer to Smith-Dorrien as 'a commander of unusual coolness, intrepidity and determination'. Five years later an embittered French was to claim that this praise was unmerited.

RIGHT
Generaloberst Karl von Einem (1853–1934), commander of VII Armeekorps. Einem succeeded Hausen in command of 3. Armee and spent the rest of the war on the Western Front. On 10 November 1918 he was appointed to command the Kronprinz's army group, but his only role was to prepare it for demobilization.

The crossing at Chezy-sur-Marne. The line of trees in the middle distance marks the course of the river. From positions like these on the north bank of the river, it was easy for the Germans to dominate the crossings.

visit each army in turn and assess its remaining fighting capacity and tactical situation. On this basis, he would then make recommendations about the general strategic situation.

Hentsch left Luxembourg at 1100hrs, first visiting the armies at the eastern end of the front. He arrived at Bülow's headquarters at 1945hrs. There he conferred straight away with General Lauenstein, 2. Armee's chief of staff, and Oberstleutnant Matthes, the chief of operations. According to Lauenstein and Matthes, 2. Armee had committed its last reserves and so was in no position to seal the breach. Hentsch was still at 2. Armee HQ when news arrived of the engagement at Marchais-en-Brie. 13. Infanterie-Division was by now falling back eastwards towards Margny, thus widening the gap even further. If this information was confirmed, the only safe course of action would have been to withdraw. But if 2. Armee withdrew on its own, the British and French forces now on the north bank of the Marne would threaten 1. Armee as well. If 2. Armee pulled back, then 1. Armee would have to follow suit.

9 September

News of the German attack on Mondement reached Franchet d'Esperey at 0715hrs. As 10e Corps d'armée was already engaged, 1er Corps d'armée was sent eastwards towards Etoges. Advancing 14km (9 miles), it encountered little resistance. But it could not move fast enough to cut X Armeekorps' line of retreat. 3e Corps d'armée now moved to fill the gap caused by 1er Corps d'armée's sideways move. It too met little resistance as it advanced towards the Marne crossing at Dormans. Around 1600hrs a German rearguard around Margny provided some opposition, but artillery quickly suppressed it. Meanwhile 18e Corps d'armée moved northwards. In possession of Château-Thierry by midday, it then took up positions on the north bank of the Marne, covering the town.

The German retreat to the Aisne, 10–11 September 1914

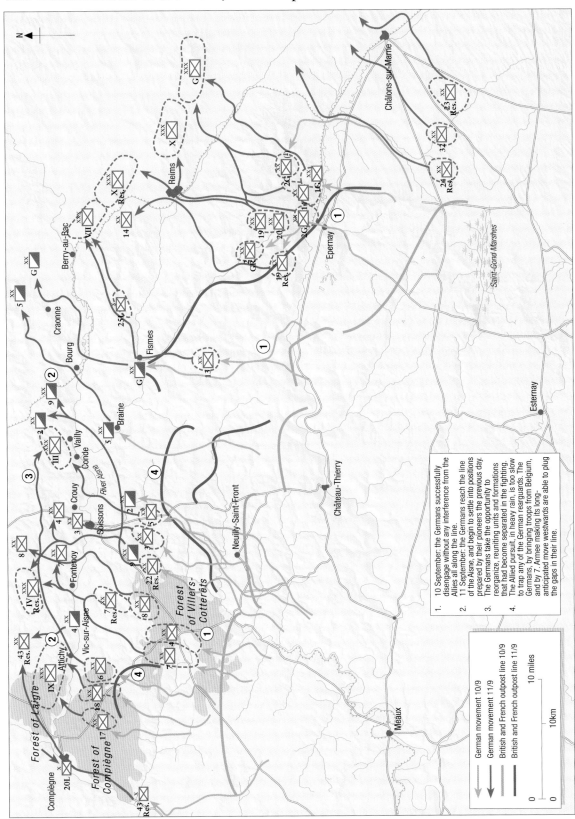

1. 10 September: the Germans successfully disengage without any interference from the Allies all along the line.
2. 11 September: the Germans reach the line of the Aisne, and begin to settle into positions prepared by their pioneers the previous day. The Germans take the opportunity to reorganize, reuniting units and formations that had become separated in the fighting.
3. The Allied pursuit, in heavy rain, is too slow to trap any of the German rearguards. The Germans, by bringing troops from Belgium, and by 7. Armee making its long-anticipated move westwards are able to plug the gaps in their line.

German movement 10/9
German movement 11/9
British and French outpost line 10/9
British and French outpost line 11/9

0   10 miles
0   10km

The remains of a retreating German convoy, caught by artillery fire near Villers-Cotterêts. Given the speed and distances involved in the German advance, the small number of motor transport columns were the only units capable of keeping the German right-wing formations supplied with ammunition.

Meanwhile the British were moving forwards slowly. French and British intelligence had greatly underestimated the speed of the German withdrawal, and Sir John French had therefore ordered his men to advance with caution. But when advance guards approached the bridges at Nogent and Azy, downstream of Château-Thierry, around 0530hrs, they found the enemy gone and were able to secure the crossings without any difficulty. At Charly-sur-Marne, 1st King's Regiment were preparing to rush the bridge:

> Then in the fields below appeared a string of dots slowly advancing towards [it]. They were a battalion sent forward to find out what there was in front of us. Every moment we expected to hear the stillness of the morning broken by the crackle of machine guns and rifle fire. They reached the bank and lay down; nothing happened. Then a figure got up and started across the bridge; surely it was mined? No! One by one they followed their leader, and started to throw the carts which formed the barricade into the river. And so we crossed absolutely unopposed; we learnt that the enemy had got everything ready for defending the bridge, and had then got hopelessly drunk.

As they moved forwards, the tired Allied soldiers were pleased to see signs of the rapid German departure. Corporal Bill Holbrook of 4th Royal Fusiliers later remembered '… the stuff they pinched, cars, lorries, even stuff they'd pinched from the Belgians, they had to leave on the side of the road because they couldn't get them back fast enough.'

Others experienced rather different emotions. An officer of 20e RD recalled:

> In the middle of the smoking ruins [of a village], amongst the blackened walls of what were houses, there were a few things left behind that typified the Teutonic soldiery. The German soldiers were absolutely gorged. We found them sprawled in very corner, on every roadside, dead drunk. Through open

windows we could see beds upside down, filthy torn mattresses, cupboards smashed with axes, their contents spilled all over. Everywhere were piles of linen, glasses and crockery, all in pieces. They had sacked everything for sheer pleasure. It was stunning and revolting. I could not believe cavalrymen had done it. In every army in the world, cavalry behave differently, with a completely different spirit. There were inscriptions written in chalk on the doors in German and in French. One tried to be funny: "Thanks to the wonderful French army for leaving us such a good dinner!"

When aerial reconnaissance reported substantial enemy forces outside Château-Thierry the advance of I Corps came to a halt whilst extra aircraft were sent to make further investigations. The all-clear was given around 1500hrs, but then 8e Division d'infanterie, which had acted as the link between 6e Armée and the British left, was withdrawn from Meaux to bolster 6e Armée's front and Sir John ordered a halt once more.

Further west, at Nanteuil and Saacy, II Corps had also succeeded in crossing the Marne during the course of the morning without much opposition. However, a battlegroup built around General Kraewel's brigade (17. Infanterie-Division, IX Armeekorps) held the opposite heights in some strength and prevented them from advancing far on the north bank. This held up progress for both 3rd and 5th Divisions until the last German position was winkled out by howitzer fire around 1800hrs.

Further west still, around La Ferté-sous-Jouarre, the advance of III Corps was held up by enfilading fire from the opposite bank in a deep bend in the river. Attempts to rush the bridge, which still survived intact, were driven off by German machine guns. Eventually, a small party of 2nd Essex Regiment found an undefended crossing at a weir and the German position was turned. However, German artillery kept British gains to a minimum and, despite the best efforts of the engineers, it was impossible to repair the damaged bridge or erect a replacement that afternoon.

The BEF requested French assistance in turning the whole position and two cavalry divisions crossed at Azy to join 18e Corps d'armée at Château-Thierry around 1700hrs. The British advance had been slow. Maunoury had requested an attack against the left rear of 1. Armee and was particularly disappointed that it never materialized. An opportunity to deal a significant blow to the Germans had been missed. But the French cavalry performed little better. Franchet d'Esperey had given Conneau a formal order to cross the Marne at Azy, with instructions to act vigorously against the retreating Germans and help 18e Corps d'armée cross the river. But the speed of the cavalry never exceeded that of their accompanying infantry: 10e Division de cavalerie – four regiments of dragoons and two of chasseurs à cheval – managed just 7km (4 miles) in two hours.

After conferring again with 2. Armee staff, Hentsch left for 1. Armee at 0700hrs. German aerial reconnaissance reported Allied columns crossing the Petit Morin and advancing on the Marne. For Bülow there was no alternative. He had to start pulling back, aiming to cross the Marne around Epernay. He ordered his right to move north-eastwards and cross around Damery; X Armeekorps was to pass through Epernay itself; and the Garde was to hold the southern approaches to the crossing.

Hentsch finally reached 1. Armee HQ at 1230hrs. The journey had not been a long one as the crow flies – only 80km (50 miles). But it had taken over five hours and Hentsch must have found the experience extremely disheartening – passing through columns of retreating or wounded troops with the threat, real or imagined, of British cavalry on the other side of every hill. As soon as he arrived, he spoke to 1. Armee's chief of staff, General Kuhl. Kuhl was appalled at what he heard. He knew 1. Armee was winning its own particular battle – the fighting that morning had driven the French left flank back some distance – and he could see no reason to withdraw. But, with the current position of 2. Armee, and the BEF now across the Marne in numbers, 1. Armee was threatened with encirclement. News that Bülow was going to withdraw decided the matter. Hentsch suggested that 1. Armee should pull back north-eastwards via Fismes in order to close the gap between 1. and 2. Armeen, but this involved a march across the front of the BEF and Kuhl declared it impossible. With Hentsch's approval, they eventually settled on a northerly route via Soissons.

AFTERMATH

A ceremony at the memorial to the 'Armies of Paris', between Penchard and Chambry. Army engineers originally created the memorial on the orders of Général Gallieni. A small ceremony was held here every year.

Most officers and men shared Kuhl's view: the order to retreat sent shock waves throughout the three German armies. All post-war accounts, official and unofficial, insist that units were nowhere near as worn out as their generals believed them to be. Nevertheless, the Germans successfully disengaged 1., 2. and 3. Armeen from the peril facing them on the Marne and retreated behind the line of the river Aisne.

While Joffre pressed forwards on the left, the French had remained on the defensive across the rest of the line. On the French right, 2e Armée (Castelnau) had come under immense pressure before the battle. On 5 September Castelnau contacted Joffre with bad news. He might have to withdraw before the German attack. Joffre asked Castelnau if he could hold for 24 hours. But there was no let-up and the following day – his judgement perhaps clouded by news that his son had been lost in action – Castelnau ordered his men to fall back. Joffre was having none of it. Immediately countermanding the order, he asked Castelnau for another 24 hours. Fortunately for Joffre – and the outcome of the battle of the Marne – German pressure slackened and the line held.

In the centre 4e Armée (Langle de Cary) and 3e Armée (Sarrail) faced a desperate struggle to hold the enemy and prevent them from piercing an irretrievably large hole in the French line. 4. and 5. Armeen were looking to strike south-eastwards, aiming to break through the heavily fortified Meuse Valley. Again Verdun was the key. On 8 September 5e Armée launched a strong attack against the fort of Troyon, guarding the southern approaches

TOP

British publishers also sought to meet popular demand for images of the conflict. This posed photograph of men of the Queen's Regiment, supposedly in action near Meaux, would be more convincing as an action shot if the corporal, standing second from the right, were not smiling.

BOTTOM

The monument at Mondement. Its base includes carved figures of Joffre and his commanders, including Sir John French. But larger than most of the generals is the figure of an ordinary soldier.

to the fortress city. Sarrail remained determined to hold on to Verdun at all costs – even if this resulted in a German breakthrough on his left. But Joffre had other ideas. He felt it more important for Sarrail to maintain contact with 4e Armée and keep the French line intact. That evening he gave Sarrail permission to withdraw. But the forts around the city held – even though the French line was eventually bent back on itself on both sides of the Meuse – and the German attacks were repulsed.

Further south the Germans were also trying hard to separate 3e Armée from 4e. Around Vitry-le-François elements of their 3. and 4. Armeen attacked in search of Langle de Cary's flanks, driving the French back from the town and opening a hole in the right of their line. This was the moment when Foch asked for help on his front – to no avail. Langle de Cary needed every man he could find to bolster his own flagging forces. But that evening the crisis passed and Langle de Cary was able to join up with Sarrail once more.

When Hentsch returned to OHL, Moltke still had hopes of limiting the retreat to 1. and 2. Armeen. Capturing Verdun would help to cover any movement on the right. On 10 September a new assault was launched – and for a time the city was nearly cut off. But the key to limiting the retreat lay in the position of the hard-pressed 3. Armee – now pulled back on the right and forward on the left. On 11 September Moltke finally left Luxembourg to visit his army HQs. He found Hausen sick, his men exhausted, and the French advance about to strike the very centre of 3. Armee. Moltke felt he had no alternative, he had to order a general retreat. In the west and centre the German armies would contract and fall back to the Aisne. In the east they would fall back in front of Nancy and to the south.

In the aftermath of the battle, Joffre's orders were unequivocal: 'To affirm and exploit [this] success, it is necessary to pursue the enemy energetically and leave him no respite: victory depends on the legs of our infantry.' But these were tired legs indeed. All they could do was follow the retreating Germans. The Allies eventually managed to gain toeholds on the north bank of the Aisne. But their positions were dominated from the higher ground occupied by the Germans. Despite several attempts, they were unable to dislodge the enemy. Under very heavy fire from German artillery, shelter trenches were dug. And from these small beginnings grew a way of warfare that would endure for another four years.

CONCLUSION

The Schlieffen Plan, as modified by Moltke, was always a gamble. It made little provision for the unexpected, relied upon meeting little or no Belgian resistance and discounted the contribution of the British. More significantly, it was far too ambitious – both in the sheer physical effort required of the German soldier and in the extent of the logistical support needed to keep him supplied. The dogged resistance put up by the French also came as a surprise. As Kluck later remarked: 'that men who had retreated for ten solid days, and who lay on the ground half-dead with fatigue, yet would pick up their weapon and charge to the sound of the bugle, is one thing we never thought would happen.'

During and immediately after the war nationalist politicians (including the influential Ludendorff, former First Quartermaster-General of the Army) fostered a particular view of the conflict. Germany's soldiers had remained undefeated in the field. They were let down instead by politicians and by feeble leadership in the early years of the conflict. Accounts of the battle of the Marne written at this time were coloured by this belief – painting it not as a defeat but rather as a victory squandered by premature retreat. And, in Moltke and Hentsch, scapegoats were readily to hand. Moltke had died, worn out, in 1916; Hentsch, following an operation, in 1917.

But, while failings in leadership and command were all too evident, the Germans had suffered a very real defeat. By breaching the gap between 1. and 2. Armeen, the Allies had made the German position untenable. Threatened with encirclement, 1. and 2. Armeen had no option but to withdraw, and once they withdrew – and renewed assaults on Verdun had failed – the other German armies had no option but to conform.

That gap had largely been created by the actions of Kluck. Ignoring Moltke's orders of 2 September, he had plunged on southwards across the

TOP

The memorial at La Ferté-sous-Jouarre commemorates nearly 4,000 officers and men of the BEF who were killed between August and early October 1914 but have no known grave. Behind the memorial is the site of the pontoon bridge across the Marne erected by the advancing British in September 1914. The graves of British soldiers who died in the battle can be found in the CWGC cemeteries at Montreuil-aux-Lions, Perreuse Château and Vailly.

BOTTOM

Prisoners were taken on both sides. Here a mixture of French and British prisoners is paraded for the camera at the prisoner-of-war transit camp at Wahn, near Cologne.

Marne with the aim of enveloping 5e Armée. Then, when he came under attack on the Ourcq, his concern lay with protecting his own right. By withdrawing two corps from Bülow's right flank, he left 2. Armee totally exposed.

In the event, it was Kluck's headstrong reaction, abandoning 2. Armee without reference to either Moltke or Bülow, as much as the French assault, that dislocated the whole German strategy. Back in Luxembourg, Moltke was too far away from the battlefield to correct this decision. Nor could he bolster Bülow, either by transferring men from another sector – since they were fixed by the French right and centre – or simply by encouraging him to hold on.

The German system of command allowed considerable discretion to the commander on the ground. Kluck, therefore, considered his behaviour nothing more than an appropriate use of initiative. But this system needed a strong supreme commander to ensure his subordinates all conformed to the overall campaign strategy. And Moltke was not that man. According to Kronprinz Rupprecht's chief of staff, Moltke 'practised an exaggerated restraint, because he... lacked all self-assurance and thus all self-confidence. He was afraid to lead by himself.'

Unlike Joffre, Moltke commanded all the German forces in the field – in two widely separated theatres, as well as at home. This had played its part in dictating the choice of Luxembourg as OHL's HQ. And, in these circumstances, a different command structure might also have served him better. A theatre commander – or perhaps two army group commanders in the west – could have concentrated on the detail of the campaign, leaving Moltke in charge of the overall coordination of strategy.

When the Allies attacked into the gap between 1. and 2. Armeen, the only troops available to oppose the advance were the two cavalry corps. When these two corps fell back they naturally retreated towards their parent formations – defending the flanks of 1. and 2. Armeen, but not actually plugging the gap. An overall commander closer to the front line would surely have been better able to coordinate his forces.

Other factors contributed to Germany's defeat. Although the Germans had succeeded in bringing their opponents to battle, they had failed to fix all the enemy forces. This allowed the Allies to regroup behind the Marne, and Joffre to use his interior lines of communication to reconcentrate his forces and outflank Kluck. Failures in operational intelligence also played their part. Had Kluck been aware of the strength and whereabouts of 6e Armée and the BEF, he would surely not have been quite so willing to plunge on with his advance. And his decision to withdraw the two corps guarding 2. Armee's right flank was also based on a misapprehension. Generalmajor Kuhl, 1. Armee's chief of staff, noted as much at the time: '… had 2. Armee been faced with a strong enemy, then IX Armeekorps would have been allowed to remain where it was.'

German strategy was based around achieving a rapid victory against the French, before transferring men and resources to deal with Russia. But, in practice, this proved impossible. The Russian Army was quicker into the field than expected. And pressure from the east deprived Moltke of two corps that might otherwise have filled the gaps soon to be apparent in the west. Moltke attracted much criticism for this decision. The German victory at Tannenberg shortly thereafter completely neutralized the Russian threat and quickly made the move irrelevant. But that was to be wise after the event. At the time Moltke had little option. Prittwitz, the German commander in the east, was under threat of encirclement and about to retreat. This would have been a catastrophic blow to German morale, leaving the important agricultural resources of East Prussia at the mercy of the advancing Russians, and Berlin (and Vienna) open to attack. Sacking Prittwitz, replacing him with Hindenburg, and providing the new commander with fresh troops can be viewed only as a reasonable response to imminent danger.

Defeat on the Marne meant that Germany's strategy lay in ruins. Its military planners were now faced with the war on two fronts they had tried so hard to avoid. But there was no contingency plan, no alternative when things went wrong. His health shattered, Moltke was sacked and replaced by Erich Falkenhayn, the Prussian minister of war. As Falkenhayn later remarked, 'Schlieffen's notes [had] come to an end, and with it, Moltke's wits.'

The part played by Hentsch in the German retreat also received much scrutiny. His role was obscured by the fact that Moltke had given him no written orders, only verbal instructions. Controversy regarding their exact nature arose almost immediately, and the clamour for an explanation continued until the spring of 1917, when OHL finally ordered an inquiry. Hentsch was able to give evidence, but his death shortly afterwards did nothing to halt the rumours.

Général Mangin (1866–1925), commander of 5e Division d'infanterie, and one of de Maud'huy's divisional commanders. An experienced colonial soldier, Mangin was a fire-eater, known to his own men as 'The Butcher'. By 1918 he was commander of 10e Armée.

Hentsch defended himself stoutly. Ordering 1. Armee to retreat lay within the scope of his instructions. Indeed, OHL maintained a contingency plan for just such an action. Faced with the withdrawal of 2. Armee, he saw little alternative: 1. Armee had to retreat in its turn. If he was wrong, he should have been reprimanded at the time. But no such reprimand had been forthcoming. Far from it, when Moltke heard Hentsch's report, his response was reportedly one of relief: 'Thank God! It is far better than I thought.'

Hentsch also refused to accept any responsibility for the indiscipline of those formations (Richthofen's Höherer Kavallerie-Kommandeur 1 a notable culprit) that had radioed their orders and reports in clear, allowing them to be intercepted by the French. Or for the poor communication between army commanders – and between those commanders and OHL – which left Bülow short of two army corps to secure his flank.

Kluck maintained to the end that he could have defeated 6e Armée by attacking on the evening of 9 September. But he was also forced to admit that any further advance on his part would have sealed his separation from the rest of the German forces and prompted a retreat via Amiens or even Dieppe. Wounded in March 1915, he retired from active service in October of the following year.

Bülow was promoted to the rank of *Generalfeldmarschall* in January 1915. But he suffered a heart attack two months later and was allowed to retire in the following year. Hausen retired from active service on grounds of ill health on 19 September 1914; General der Kavallerie von Einem, the commander of VII Armeekorps, replaced him.

On the French side, much ink was spilled in the post-war years in the effort to establish the claims of one general or another to the victory of the Marne. Without Joffre, it would certainly have been impossible. His was the vision to hold the Germans where he did and his the unshakeable confidence that prevented the Allied armies from disintegrating. Foch commented, 'If we had not had him in 1914, I don't know what would have become of us.' Joffre put it another way. He later remarked drily, 'I don't know who won the battle, but had it been lost, then it would have been me that lost it.'

Yet without the staunch defence of 1ère and 2e Armées on the Moselle, there would have been no position for Joffre to hold. Without Gallieni's quick wit, the opportunity for Maunoury's attack might have been lost. Without Lanrezac's victory at Guise on 29 August, the French Army would not have had the time to recover. And without the drive of Foch and Franchet d'Esperey, the defence of the Saint-Gond marshes and the advance into the gap between 1. and 2. Armeen would not have been possible.

But, for all the heat generated by the controversy, the battle of the Marne remained a flawed victory. True, the invading armies had been turned back. But it had proved impossible to deal them a decisive blow. Indeed, they continued to occupy a considerable part of northern France, including the important coal and steel region of Briey, in Alsace. Pursuit of the retreating Germans had simply been not vigorous enough. Much of this can be explained by the rigours of the preceding campaign, which took its toll of men and animals alike. But this was not the whole story. Conneau's Corps de cavalerie was unable to advance decisively into the gap between 1. and 2. Armeen – not only through exhaustion but also because its horses were poorly cared for. It seems unlikely that this would have happened under a Murat.

Indeed, leaders with the all-round ability of Murat were few and far between in the French Army of the period. Individual initiative was discouraged, and

German prisoners from RIR 36 stand outside the church at Neufmontiers, a mounted provost guard to their right.

Joffre was able to keep a much tighter rein on his subordinates than could Moltke. Liaison officers at each army headquarters acted as a conduit for reports and guidance between GQG and the front, ensuring that army commanders followed orders.

But this system was not guaranteed to produce general officers of the calibre required. Joffre did not hesitate to sack a number of senior officers whose performance was not up to standard. By the end of the battle of the Marne, two army commanders, ten corps commanders and perhaps as many as 38 divisional commanders had all felt Joffre's wrath – their careers 'put at the disposition of the Minister'. A few eventually received another field command. But the majority were shunted into administrative posts in the regions, or simply retired.

Hailed as the 'Victor of the Marne', Joffre could for a time do no wrong in the eyes of politicians and public alike. But in 1916, his reputation tarnished by failure to inflict a decisive defeat on the Germans, he was removed from command. Created a marshal of France, he was given a largely sinecure post within the Ministry of War. Joffre's army commanders met with varying fortunes. Franchet d'Esperey became an army group commander in 1915, before being appointed commander of the Allied forces in Salonika in 1918. Maunoury was badly wounded in 1915 – eventually losing his sight – and was appointed military governor of Paris in the same year. Foch was promoted to army group commander in 1915, his star then waning with Joffre's fall. But he rose again and was appointed to supreme command of all the Allied Forces in 1918. Gallieni remained in his post of military governor of Paris until October 1915, when he was appointed minister of war. Ill health and disillusion with politics and politicians prompted his retirement in January 1916, and he died in May of that year.

Other relatively minor actors in the drama of the Marne went on to greater things. Pétain and Mangin – both divisional commanders in 5e Armée – became army commanders. Pétain went on to become the hero of Verdun and play a significant part in World War II. Robert Nivelle, the 6e Armée artillery colonel whose batteries had alone defeated a German attack, received

German prisoners boarding a train on the outskirts of Paris. Prisoner-of-war camps were situated all over France, but especially in the south-west, and on the Atlantic coast.

a brigade on the back of his performance. His subsequent rise was swift, and his fall equally so. Replacing Joffre in overall command of French armies on the Western Front in December 1916, he was sacked ignominiously the following summer after the failure of his Spring Offensive. Alphonse Juin, in 1914 a young officer in the Brigade Marocaine, would lose an arm the following year. But he went on to become commander of the Corps Expéditionnaire Français fighting in Italy in 1943–44 and a marshal of France.

Accurate casualty figures for the battle of the Marne are hard to obtain. Many units submitted irregular returns at this time – to the despair of the French Official History – so precise figures for the battle itself are impossible to establish. The Official History offers figures only for the whole of September, which must, of course, include the later fighting on the Aisne. In this period the French lost a total of 213,445 men: 18,073 killed, 111,963 wounded and 83,409 missing.

Regimental depots were scoured for every available man to replace the losses. The class of 1914 had already been called up on the outbreak of war and this would eventually yield some 292,447 men. In December 1914, the class of 1915 was called up as well, adding a further 279,112 new recruits. The Sultan of Morocco sent another regiment. And more men were sought from those French regiments serving in North Africa.

As far as the British were concerned, Sir John French's time in command was not always a happy one. A gifted cavalry leader, as he showed in South Africa, the campaigns of 1914–15 showed him out of his depth with the full panoply of modern warfare. He appeared to be weighed down by the responsibility of commanding his country's main field force and he was an often-unwilling partner to the French. One contemporary politician said of him, 'I daresay that he is not the cleverest man, but he is the most successful soldier we could find.' He was eventually sacked in December 1915, after the battle of Loos.

Wounded German prisoners, guarded by gendarmes, rest in the field hospital at Varreddes after the German retreat.

French's relationship with his subordinates was often quarrelsome. French and Smith-Dorrien had clashed before the outbreak of war – largely over the role of cavalry in modern warfare – and Smith-Dorrien's last-minute appointment to II Corps had been made against French's express wishes. Their feud continued to flare up at the front until the spring of 1915, when French succeeded in having Smith-Dorrien removed, perhaps unfairly, from command.

Of the other British commanders, Pulteney – despite his apparent incompetence – remained in post until 1918, when he was sacked after the German Spring Offensive. Both Allenby and Gough became army commanders during the course of the war. Allenby became Allied commander in Palestine. However, Gough, like Pulteney, was made to shoulder responsibility for the poor British performance of March 1918.

According to the British Official History, British casualties in the battle totalled 12,733. The first drafts of reservists were joining their battalions in France just as the battle began, and others were on their way to France. But manpower remained low for the rest of the year. The 'New Army' of men who had volunteered on the outbreak of war was as yet nowhere near fully trained. Meanwhile the Territorial Force was deemed suitable only for garrison duties. Immediate reinforcements had to come from India, with the first two divisions arriving in October.

German casualty figures are equally difficult to establish. The German Official History of the battle provides none and many army papers were destroyed during World War II. In the semi-official *Schlachten des Weltkrieges*, casualties in the infantry divisions of 1. Armee are given as 422 officers and 11,320 men. The brunt of these was borne by IV Reservekorps, which lost 189 officers and 4,502 men. However, even these figures are incomplete, and do not include many of the artillery regiments.

Losses were certainly severe in some 1. Armee regiments. Infanterie-Regiment 165 lost 22 officers and 606 men. Meanwhile, in Reservekorps, four infantry regiments lost around one third of their total strength – over 600 men each. 2. Armee's losses totalled 396 officers and 12,369 men, while those of the 3. Armee formations engaged along the Somme were 91 officers and 5,107 men.

The Gardekorps was the hardest hit of all the formations engaged anywhere in the battle, losing 179 officers and 5,748 men. The Franz and Augusta regiments were almost halved in strength, each losing over 900 all ranks, while the other two regiments lost over 800 each. Across all the armies most heavily engaged during the battle, the Saxon Official Historian Generalmajor Baumgarten-Crusius estimated that fully two-thirds of regimental officers had been killed or wounded. In addition, the French claimed 40,000 prisoners. However, this figure must include some of the wounded from the totals above – those deemed too badly injured to be moved and thus left behind during the retreat.

The class of 1914 reported in September of that year. But the class of 1915 was not called up until the following spring – between April and June. During September 1914 the Germans turned to a mixture of untrained volunteers, reservists and older men from the Landwehr and Landsturm to fill the gaps. In November 1914 these corps took part in the first battle of Ypres. But, with so little time to train, they incurred heavy losses.

The French artillery played an important part in the battle – but not in the role intended by the regulations. Poor coordination with the infantry meant that many attacks were unsupported by the artillery and heavy casualties were incurred as a result. It was not that the artillery turned its back on bombarding enemy positions. Indeed, these tactics were successful in halting many German attacks. But the rate at which equipment and shells were used provoked a crisis. At mobilization 530,000 rounds of 75mm ammunition were available; by 5 September stocks had fallen to 465,000; and by 10 September only 33,000 remained. Reserve magazines, which normally held 300 rounds per gun, were empty. Some armies were using ammunition for the heavier 120L cannon at the rate of 62 shells a day. Yet the factories were turning out only four shells a day. Nor could the magazines keep up with the demand for replacement weapons. On 10 September the seven French armies had a total deficit of 272 guns and 713 caissons. Of these, only 120 guns and 346 caissons could be replaced immediately.

This was not the only cause for concern. Before the war the French had made the decision to concentrate on field artillery at the expense of heavier calibres and howitzers – a policy whose flaws were quickly revealed by the performance of the German artillery on the Marne. The 155 CTR, the only heavy piece of field artillery in the French arsenal, had soon proved itself inaccurate. To make up the deficit Joffre had to make do and mend. He got hold of naval guns and stripped older weapons from coastal fortifications and from the fortresses at Lyon, Grenoble and Briançon. Given how easily the

Germans had taken strongholds like Liège, this seemed a sensible measure. But it was a decision that would return to haunt the French at Verdun.

Overall, though, German soldiers were impressed with the accuracy and volume of French fire. And post-war accounts compared it favourably with their own. Writing in 1920, Generalleutnant Rohne admitted: 'French field artillery was superior to ours not only from the point of view of equipment, but also in its employment and the weight of the bombardment.' French artillery certainly outranged the German equivalent, their shrapnel shells had a wider bursting radius, and their high-explosive shells were more powerful. 'It is sad to recall,' concluded Baumgarten-Crusius, 'that despite the excellent training of men and horses, imbued as they all were with such a proud spirit compared to the French, at the beginning of the war the German artillery was not at the top of its game.'

If one aspect of the battle presaged the shape of things to come, it was the role of aerial reconnaissance. Before the outbreak of war, Général Foch had dismissed aircraft as good for sport and nothing else. Yet it was aircraft that spotted Kluck's turn away from Paris, and further missions, on both sides, kept a close eye on the ground forces as they manoeuvred for advantage. The comparative failure of the cavalry placed the achievement of aerial reconnaissance in particularly high relief, but it was not an unalloyed success. Aviation officers were not yet skilled in interpreting what they saw, and the generals on the ground had not yet learnt to trust the results. It was this gap between the ability to perceive the enemy's movements and to comprehend fully their implications that induced caution, sometimes overcaution, in commanders – particularly on the Allied side. Yet before long aircraft would become an integral weapon in the arsenal of both combatants.

THE BATTLEFIELD TODAY

Although some areas are now more heavily wooded than in 1914, the battlefield is little changed and still produces a heavy crop of cereals and sugar beet. In the west the railway line of the TGV Est cuts across the fields where 55e Division de réserve strove in vain to reach the German lines. Here, near Chambry, a French war cemetery and a German war cemetery lie on opposite sides of a line that now connects Paris with Strasbourg and Stuttgart. In the eastern part of the battlefield, the busy N4 snakes its way around Esternay, Sézanne and Fère-Champenoise, while the small airport of Châlons-Vatry occupies the fields crossed by the Saxons in their attack on Lenharrée.

After the war a number of monuments were erected in and around the battlefield to commemorate the Allied victory. A squat block in honour of the 'Armies of Paris', placed by a dusty crossroads near Penchard, is now bypassed by the modern road system. A monument to Gallieni was placed curiously distant from the battlefield – near Trilbardou, west of Meaux. The statue has now been stolen, so the monument consists only of a plinth. A modernist mosaic marks the grave of the writer Charles Péguy – killed in front of Villeroy

The memorial to the fighting at Mondement towers over the village church. Although authorized by parliament in 1920, the design competition did not take place until 1929. In the following year the commission was handed to Paul Bigot and Henri Bouchard. The monolith was in place in 1933, but its carvings were not finished until just before the outbreak of war in 1939, lending a certain irony to its motto 'To all who since time immemorial have stood up against those who would invade our land'.

on the first day of the battle – as well as 98 of his comrades from 231e, 246e and 276e RIs. A small column in the churchyard of Lenharrée was erected by the villagers in honour of the 540 Frenchmen who fell defending their home. And, most extraordinary of all, a granite and concrete menhir at Mondement, 33m (108ft) high, looks out from the ridge over the Saint-Gond marshes. Two more monuments were built at the initiative of local clergy: Notre Dame de la Marne, near Barcy, built in 1924; and the chapel on a hill overlooking the small town of Dormans, built between 1921 and 1931, which commemorates both the first and second battles of the Marne.

At the time of writing, there are two small museums devoted to the battle, at Villeroy and at Mondement; both concentrate on the fighting in the local area. A new museum of the Great War is planned for Meaux, opening in 2011.

FURTHER READING

Baumgarten-Crusius, Artur, *Deutsche Heerführung im Marne Feldzug 1914* Scherl: Berlin, 1922

Bidwell, Shelford, and Graham, Dominick, *Fire-power: British Army Weapons and Theories of War 1904–1945* Allen & Unwin: London, 1982

Bircher, Eugen, *Krisis an der Marneschlacht* Bircher: Berlin, 1927

Breguet, Emmanuel and Claude, 'La reconnaissance aérienne et la bataille de la Marne (30 août–3 septembre 1914)', *Revue historique des armées*, 166, pp. 92–100, 1987

Bülow, Karl von, *Mein Bericht zur Marneschlacht* Scherl: Berlin, 1919

Chambe, General René, *Adieu, cavalerie!: la Marne, bataille gagnée, victoire perdue* Plon: Paris, 1979

Dahlmann, Reinhold et al., *Das Marnedrama 1914: Schlachten des Weltkrieges Vols. 22–26* Oldenburg: Stalling, 1928

Doughty, Robert A., *Pyrrhic Victory: French Strategy and Operations in the Great War* Harvard: Cambridge, Mass., 2005

Edmonds, James, *Military Operations France and Belgium 1914: Volume 1* Macmillan: London, 1933

French Army, *Les armées françaises dans la grande guerre: Volume 1* Imprimerie Nationale: Paris, 1922–37

Hanotaux, Gabriel, *La bataille de la Marne* Plon: Paris, 1922

Hausen, Max von, *Erinnerungen an den Marnefeldzug 1914* Koehler: Leipzig, 1922

Isselin, Bernard, *La bataille de la Marne* Arthaud: Paris, 1960

Kluck, Alexander von, *Der Marsch auf Paris und die Marneschlacht 1914* Mittler: Berlin, 1920

Macdonald, Lyn, *1914: the Days of Hope* Penguin: London, 1989

Michelin & Co., *Guide to the Battlefields of the Marne* Michelin: London, 1919

Mombauer, Annika, *Helmuth von Moltke and the Origins of the First World War* Cambridge University Press: Cambridge, 2005

Mueller-Loebnitz, Wilhelm, *Die Sendung des Oberstleutnants Hentsch am 8–10 September 1914* Reichsarchiv: Berlin, 1922

Oxford Dictionary of National Biography Oxford University Press: Oxford, 2004

Reichsarchiv, *Der Weltkrieg 1914–1918: die Militärischen Operationen zu Lande Vol. 4: die Marnefeldzug: die Schlacht* Mittler: Berlin, 1922

Ritter, Gerhard, *The Schlieffen Plan: Critique of a Myth* Wolff: London, 1958

Soudagne, Jean-Pascal, *Les taxis de la Marne Editions* Ouest-France: Rennes, 2008

Spears, E. L., *Liaison 1914* Heinemann: London, 1930

Strachan, Hew, *The First World War: Vol. 1 To Arms* Oxford University Press: Oxford, 2001

Tuchman, Barbara, *August 1914* Macmillan: London, 1980

Villate, Robert, 'L'Etat matériel des armées allemandes en août et septembre 1914', *Revue d'histoire de la guerre mondiale*, 4, pp. 310–27, 1926

Villate, Robert, *Foch à la Marne: la 9e armée aux marais de Saint-Gond, 5–10 septembre 1914* Lavauzelle: Paris, 1933

Zuber, Terence, *Battle of the Frontiers: Ardennes 1914* Tempus: Stroud, 2008

——, *Inventing the Schlieffen Plan* Oxford University Press: Oxford, 2002

French, British and German war diaries and regimental histories

INDEX

NEW VANGUARD • 169

US FAST BATTLESHIPS 1936–47

The North Carolina and South Dakota classes

LAWRENCE BURR   ILLUSTRATED BY PETER BULL

First published in Great Britain in 2010 by Osprey Publishing,
PO Box 883, Oxford, OX1 9PL, UK
PO Box 3985, New York, NY 10185-3985, USA
Email: info@ospreypublishing.com

Osprey Publishing is part of the Osprey Group.

Transferred to digital print on demand 2014.

First published 2010
3rd impression 2011

Printed and bound by PrintOnDemand-Worldwide.com, Peterborough, UK.

A CIP catalog record for this book is available from the British Library.

ISBN: 978 1 84603 510 4
E-book ISBN: 978 1 84908 292 1

Page layout by Melissa Orrom Swan, Oxford
Index by Mike Parkin
Typeset in Sabon and Myriad Pro
Originated by PPS Grasmere Ltd, Leeds, UK

Author's acknowledgments
The author wishes to acknowledge the help and assistance of the following: Captain Ben
W. Blee, USN (Ret); Jeffrey Nilsson, Executive Director, Historical Naval Ships Association;
Kim Sincox, Museum Services Director, and Mary Ames Booker, Curator of Collections,
Battleship North Carolina; Bill Tunnell, Executive Director, and Lee Bryars, Crew Chief,
Museum USS Alabama; Mark Hayes, Naval Historical Center; Professor Douglas V. Smith,
Naval War College; Captain Christopher Page (RN) Ret, and Dr Malcolm Llewellyn-Jones,
Historian, Naval Historical Branch; Ron Kurpiers, researcher; and my wonderful wife Judi,
whose patience and humor helped me cope with a new computer.

Photographic credits
All the photographs printed in this book are by: Courtesy Battleship North Carolina.

The Woodland Trust
Osprey Publishing is supporting the Woodland Trust, the UK's leading woodland
conservation charity, by funding the dedication of trees.

www.ospreypublishing.com

CONTENTS

US FAST BATTLESHIPS 1936–47
THE NORTH CAROLINA AND SOUTH DAKOTA CLASSES

INTRODUCTION

The six battleships of the North Carolina and South Dakota classes, built between 1937 and 1942, represented a dramatic development from the pre-1922 battleships of the US Navy. The Washington Naval Treaty (WNT) of 1922 and the resulting battleship-building "holiday" stopped the gradual development process of battleship design that had flowed from the launching of the British HMS *Dreadnought* in 1905. In 1937, US Navy designers had to set a design within three fixed parameters: the width of the Panama Canal, a maximum displacement of 35,000 tons, and a maximum main armament caliber of 16 inches. The designed speed of 27 knots for these six battleships was set on the basis of faulty intelligence of the speed of the Japanese Kongo class of fast battleships of 26 knots.

The design of the North Carolina and South Dakota class battleships was very successful. Although their service life was relatively short (all six fast battleships were decommissioned in 1947), they undertook a multiplicity of roles in both the Atlantic and Pacific theaters of war, and helped forge a new war-winning weapon system. This book tells the story of how these ships came into being and how they were used in World War II.

THE WASHINGTON NAVAL TREATY – 1922

> "*The United States of America, the British Empire, France, Italy and Japan: Desiring to contribute to the maintenance of the general peace, and to reduce the burden of competition in armament;*"
> Introduction to the Washington Naval Treaty, signed on February 6, 1922.

The purpose of the WNT was to curtail the developing naval race between the US, Great Britain, and Japan, and thereby allow the US, and Great Britain in particular, to recover financially from World War I. The cost of new fleets of battleships was seen as politically and financially prohibitive in a war-weary environment at the conclusion of the "War to end all Wars."

The signed treaty limited the construction of new battleships, defined as armored ships in excess of 10,000 tons, until December 1931. The subsequent London Naval Treaty of 1930 extended this limitation until 1936. Additionally, the WNT limited the number of battleships for each country by establishing a total maximum standard displacement of 525,000 tons each for the US and Great Britain, 315,000 tons for Japan and 175,000 tons each

Babcock and Wilcox high-pressure boilers being installed in *North Carolina*'s No. 2 machinery space.

for France and Italy. This was referred to as the 5-5-3-1.75-1.75 ratio. To bring the terms of the treaty into being, the US and Japan were authorized to complete two new battleships under construction. The UK was authorized to build two new battleships but their displacement was limited to 35,000 tons and their main armament caliber to 16 inches.

An immediate consequence of this treaty was the scrapping of battleships under construction and in operation to achieve the agreed ratios. For the US, it resulted in the scrapping of 15 battleships and the cancellation of 15 under construction. This left the US Navy with 18 battleships, including the two to be completed in accordance with the treaty. Additionally, two battlecruisers under construction were to be converted to aircraft carriers.

Existing battleships could be modernized to increase defense against air and submarine attack by adding side blisters and additional horizontal deck armor to a limit of 3,000 tons per ship. The sinking of *Ostfriesland*, *Virginia*, and *New Jersey* in 1921 in bombing trials led by Billy Mitchell pointed to the growing risk to battleships from aircraft.

The treaty also limited the number of aircraft carriers to a total displacement to 135,000 tons for the US and UK, 81,000 tons for Japan, and 60,000 tons each for France and Italy. The maximum displacement for each ship was 27,000 tons, with a proviso that the two US aircraft carriers, being converted from battlecruiser hulls, could be built up to 33,000 tons. All aircraft carriers in existence or being built on November 12, 1921 were considered experimental and could be replaced within the total tonnage limit. Main gun armament was limited to a caliber of 8 inches.

The treaty limitations established a maximum size for cruisers at 10,000 tons and 8-inch guns. As there was no limit placed on the number that could be built, the building of heavy cruisers became, in effect, a new naval race.

For the US Navy, the WNT achieved naval parity with the Royal Navy, then the preeminent naval power, without a costly naval building program and naval conflict (an approach with which Germany had failed). Following the treaty, Admiral Scheer, who had commanded the German High

The operating face of the high-pressure boilers, showing left and right furnaces.

Seas Fleet in 1916, perceptively commented that the US Navy was the real victor of the 1916 battle of Jutland between the Royal Navy and the German Imperial Navy. Additionally, the treaty ended the Anglo-Japanese Naval Treaty of 1902, and the potential alliance of the Royal Navy with the Imperial Japanese Navy (IJN) against the US Navy in the Pacific. This was significant to the US, as war scares with Japan in the early 1900s had resulted in the Naval War College (NWC) creating a War Plan "Orange" to identify the major issues and required strategy for a naval campaign against Japan. The passage of the Great White Fleet across the Pacific in 1907 was an exercise to help identify the issues involved in a trans-Pacific voyage by the fleet, as well as showing the Japanese US naval strength.

Japan had not been successful in obtaining equal status with the US and UK in terms of total battleship displacement. In seeking to have naval dominance in the western Pacific Japan negotiated and achieved a "Non-Fortification Clause" that prevented naval bases in the Pacific from being developed and defended. For the US, this meant Guam, Wake, the Philippines, and the Aleutian Islands. The consequences of the "Non-Fortification Clause" gave the IJN a significant advantage in the event of hostilities with the US. The US Navy Fleet would have to pass through the Japanese mandate possessions of the Marshal, Caroline, and Mariana Islands to reinforce its fleet in the Philippines, Wake, and Guam. This would expose the US Fleet to interception and attrition tactics by the IJN, prior to an expected fleet battle. Additionally, the US Navy would have to retain ships in the Atlantic at the same time it commenced hostilities against Japan, with the result that the IJN would have an equal or larger fleet at the time of battle. The "Non-Fortification Clause" played a major role in driving the development programs of the US Navy.

The modernization program for pre-1922 battleships focused on converting coal-fired ships to oil-burning ships, enhancing fuel-storage for greater operating range, improving fire-control systems, modifying gun turrets to increase gun elevation and range, and air-borne gun spotting. The designing and building of heavy cruisers that could operate across the distances of the Pacific led to advances in marine engineering for increased power and speed with less weight.

The US Navy also commenced developing its air arm in terms of aircraft carriers, deck-loads, aircraft types and air/naval battle tactics, including the introduction of dive-bombing. Aircraft carriers were seen as mobile airfields in the absence of Pacific bases, providing air cover for the advancing fleet. The US Marines developed an amphibious doctrine for opposed landings reflecting the need of the US Navy to capture and hold Pacific islands. Additionally, the US Navy developed a logistical fleet train capability, including a floating dry-dock to supply and repair warships as they crossed the Pacific. Annual fleet exercises, referred to as "Fleet Problems," explored the strategic and tactical issues of a trans-Pacific campaign.

While Japan felt compelled to sign the WNT, a powerful clique within the IJN led by Admiral Kato Kanji believed that Japan warranted equal ranking in terms of the size of its battleship navy in relation to the US and Great Britain. This issue and the political power of the clique grew in significance and finally resulted in Japan giving notice in 1934 of its intention to withdraw from the naval treaty system during the Second London Naval Conference beginning in January 1936.

General Electric high-pressure impulse turbine showing 12 rotary blades.

Ironically, the US Congress had prevented the US Navy from building to WNT tonnage standards until the Vinson-Trammell Act of March 1934. This Act authorized and funded the construction of 102 ships over an eight-year period to bring the US Navy up to its WNT limits.

The battleship-building holiday that lasted from 1923 until 1937 for the US Navy resulted in a dramatic change in battleship characteristics with the laying down of the new fast battleships.

DESIGN AND CONSTRUCTION

The North Carolina class

The North Carolina class battleships were the first battleships to be built in the US since the USS *West Virginia* was commissioned on December 1, 1923.

The process that led to the final design for the North Carolina class battleships had commenced in 1928, in anticipation of the WNT ending in December 1931. The extension of the building holiday clause of the WNT by the London Naval Treaty in 1930 to December 1936 took away the necessity for the design plans to be finalized. However, two critical design characteristics emerged from the 1928 design process: the 5-inch/38 caliber high-angle dual-purpose gun for secondary armament, and an evaluation of the 16-inch/50 caliber and 45 caliber main armament.

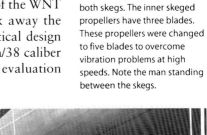

Aft view of port propellers and both skegs. The inner skeged propellers have three blades. These propellers were changed to five blades to overcome vibration problems at high speeds. Note the man standing between the skegs.

In 1931 the General Board of the US Navy, responsible for setting the basic design parameters for US warships, required an evaluation of a potential small battleship design of less than 35,000 tons armed with 12-inch guns. This small battleship concept had been suggested by the Admiralty of the Royal Navy for discussion at the next naval treaty conference planned for 1936. However, the concept was considered unacceptable to the US Navy in light of battleships, battlecruisers, and pocket battleships in service with the Royal Navy, IJN and the new German Navy, and under construction in France and Italy.

Interestingly, in 1933, the design process generated a hybrid fast battleship/aircraft carrier. The purpose of this hybrid ship was to escort and protect fast fleet carriers, with its triple armament of 12-inch or 14-inch guns, a large number of anti-aircraft (AA) guns and eight aircraft carried below deck. The displacement was suggested between 19,500 and 28,500 tons with a speed of 32.5 knots. This hybrid concept did not survive the detailed design process that commenced in 1934 and focused on the key differences between slow battleships at 21 knots and fast battleships with a speed of 30 knots.

A key consideration in this process was the assumed speed of the IJN's Kongo class of fast battleships, the *Kongo*, *Haruna*, *Hiei*, and *Kirishima*, which had been modernized following the WNT with increased armor protection from their original battlecruiser design. The speed was assumed to be 26 knots, but these ships were in fact much faster, a fact unknown to the US Navy in 1934. However, even the assumed speed of 26 knots made the Kongo class 5 knots faster than existing US battleships.

The General Board saw the need for a battleship built to treaty limits that would act as a "fast-wing" of the US battle fleet to catch the Kongo class fast battleships, as well as having the speed and endurance to hunt down and destroy the commerce raiders of Germany and Italy. This melding of battleship and Admiral Fisher's original battlecruiser concept roles established the need for and the role of a fast battleship.

General Board member Admiral Reeves argued in 1936 that the new battleships should have the same top speed, 33 knots, as fleet carriers. Admiral Reeves had driven the development of US carriers, and as captain of USS *Saratoga* during Fleet Problem IX in 1929 demonstrated the potential role of fleet carriers as Fast Task Force attack groups, operating independently of the main battle fleet. In effect this confirmed the potential as originally demonstrated by HMS *Furious* and the 1st Light Cruiser squadron in July 1918, when HMS *Furious* launched the first carrier strike of seven Sopwith Camel biplanes and destroyed German Zeppelins and their hanger base at Tondern.

However, during the period 1936/7, the final consideration for the design for the North Carolina class battleships focused on main armament and armor, with speed a secondary consideration. The WNT displacement clause

USS *NORTH CAROLINA*

The clean lines of *North Carolina*'s sweeping weather deck, and the tower superstructure topped with the massive CXAM "bedspring" radar, can be readily appreciated from the drawing of *North Carolina* as she appeared in early 1942. Her revolutionary and graceful design, with the secondary armament of 20 5-inch guns mounted in ten gun turrets, rather than in casements as in pre-1922 battleships, clearly marked her as a modern battleship in a period of increasing threat from aircraft.

This drawing of *North Carolina* depicts her as she was prior to the battle of the Eastern Solomons with 1.1-inch AA canons as the primary close-in weapon, and before "Stryker's Bridge" had been added. The battle of the Eastern Solomons showed that the AA armament was inadequate to prevent attacking aircraft from releasing either bomb or torpedo, but able to down the aircraft after the release when it was pulling out from its attacking maneuver and close in to the ship. This fact, together with the mechanical problems with the 1.1-inch canon, led to the adoption of the 40mm Bofors gun as the primary close-in AA gun that could destroy an attacking aircraft before it could release its weapon.

With four propellers and twin rudders, the *North Carolina* was very maneuverable, and able to match the gyrations of carriers as they maneuvered either to fly off and land aircraft or to dodge bombs and torpedoes. Although the first of the fast battleships, she was not fast enough to keep station with a carrier traveling at top speed of 33 knots.

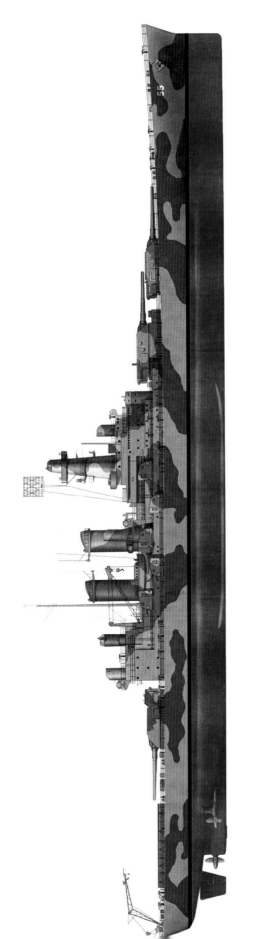
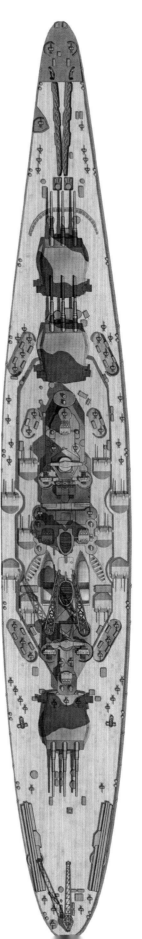

The upper rotating gun house for Turret 3 being lowered into position by the 350-ton hammerhead crane at Brooklyn Navy Yard.

Lowering a 16-inch, 45 caliber gun into the right gun house in Turret 2.

of 35,000 tons and the maximum beam that could be accommodated in the Panama Canal were the primary considerations for the designers. This led to the North Carolina class battleships having 15-degree inclined armor, four sets of lightweight geared turbines, and high-temperature high-pressure boilers, both of which were new technology. Turbines and boilers, with their respective supporting machinery, were combined in four machinery rooms rather than in separate engine and boiler rooms to provide greater survivability in the case of a torpedo hit. Between the inclined armor belt and the external hull plates were a series of watertight spaces that provided protection against torpedo blast and carried fuel and water. Together with the spaces created by the double bottom, the ships had 1.8 million gallons, or 7,167 tons, of fuel capacity for a 16,000-mile cruising range.

The balance between guns and armor originally established 12 14-inch guns in four turrets as the main armament. Secondary armament was 20 5-inch/38 guns in ten turrets. Armor protection was set to withstand hits from 14-inch guns, with an immune zone between 19,000 and 30,000 yards. The armored section of the ship extended from just forward of Turret 1 to just aft of Turret 3, thereby encompassing the magazines and machinery spaces. Finally, speed was set at 27 knots, sufficient to catch the assumed 26-knot speed of the Kongos but 6 knots slower than US fast carriers.

The Second London Naval Treaty of 1936 introduced escalator clauses to provide flexibility for signing nations, to counter the withdrawal of Japan from the naval treaty system and new battleships that Japan might build. The escalator clause covered displacement and the caliber for the main armament.

In July 1937, the Secretary of the Navy approved changing the main armament for the North Carolina class battleships from 12 14-inch to nine 16-inch/45 guns. This change was possible because the turret size for quadruple 14-inch guns was the same for triple 16-inch guns. In US Navy terms the ship was now unbalanced, in that the striking force of its guns was greater than the defensive capability of its own armor. But increases in armor protection would have increased displacement above the 35,000-ton treaty limit, and this was unacceptable.

The USS North Carolina was built at the New York Navy Yard, launched in June 1940, and commissioned in April 1941. The USS Washington was built at the Philadelphia Navy Yard, launched in June 1940, and commissioned in May 1941. Both ships experienced significant vibration along their propeller shafts and gearing and turbine machinery and the extent of this vibration adversely effected fire-control instruments. The cause of the vibration was traced to alternating thrusts emanating from inboard and outboard propellers resonating against the lightweight hull and machinery. Efforts to identify and then resolve the vibration led to the *North Carolina* sailing from and returning to the New York Navy Yard so many times that she gained the nickname "The Showboat." The problem was managed by changing the inner skeged propellers from three blades to five blades. Additionally, bracing was added to machinery. Both ships were then able to attain designed top speed at full power.

The two new "fast battleships" were very impressive, with their unbroken sweeping weather deck, pyramid tower superstructure, heavy main armament, turreted secondary armament, relatively high speed, and extensive cruising range.

The South Dakota class

Design of the South Dakota class commenced in 1937, and sought to rectify the inadequate armor design of the North Carolina class. But increasing the weight of armor and inclining side armor at 19 degrees to counter the steeper diving angle of 16-inch shells, whilst maintaining nine 16-inch guns, required significant weight savings in other areas of the ship in order to stay within the 35,000-ton limit. Additionally, these new ships were to serve as fleet and division flagships, requiring working and accommodation space for admirals and their staff.

Towards the end of designing the North Carolina class the possibility of ships sustaining underwater hull damage from steeply diving heavy shells that fell short of the ship was considered to be important. However, as the design process was so advanced, only supplemental protection for the magazines could be added. For the South Dakota class the danger from underwater shell hits was addressed and incorporated into the design to protect both magazine and machinery spaces. The inward sloping main armor belt from the armored deck was continued down to the inner bottom plates. Additionally, the strength of plates used for the outer and inner bottom plates and other internal longitudinal plates was increased relative to the North Carolina class.

A 16-inch, 45 caliber gun being installed. The two hydraulic recoil/run-out cylinders are clearly shown on the top of the gun.

In achieving the additional armor required to protect against 16-inch shells, the designers proposed a ship design of 666ft at the waterline, 47ft shorter than the North Carolina class at 713ft, in order to meet the 35,000-ton limit. As ship length equates to ship speed, the South Dakota class required increased engine power to achieve the same top speed of 27 knots as the North Carolina class. Incorporating increased engine power in a shorter hull required positioning sets of evaporators and distilling equipment into the four machinery rooms, along with the boilers and turbines, rather than into their own separate compartments. The boilers within the machinery spaces were raised one deck in order for the propeller shaft to run beneath them and thereby reduce the space required for machinery. Additionally, the bottom hull aft of the stern magazine was drastically reduced to, in turn, reduce hull drag. The two outer propellers and shafts were incorporated in skegs, creating a tunnel in which the inner two propellers were located, providing a measure of protection from torpedoes for the inner propellers.

The shortened design incorporated a single funnel into the aft section of the superstructure. *South Dakota* was fitted with eight secondary 5-inch gun turrets rather than ten, and the space for the 5-inch handling room and magazine was used to provide accommodation. The USS *Indiana*, *Massachusetts*, and *Alabama* were built with 20 5-inch/38 guns in ten turrets.

The massive bridge and conning tower, incorporating the captain's command bridge with the admiral's bridge above and main battery fire control at top level followed aft by the superstructure tower and incorporated funnel, above a sweeping weather deck, gave the class a powerful appearance. The improved armor protection made the South Dakota class a more powerful battleship in battleship-vs-battleship action than the North Carolina class.

Fire control

Whilst guns, armor, and speed are essential characteristics of battleships, the ability to hit the target with their gunfire represents the ultimate justification for the time and money spent on developing and operating them.

The North Carolina and South Dakota class battleships were all fitted with Ford Instrument Mark 8 Range Keepers. These mechanical/electric fire-control analog computers were the latest development starting with the Stadimeter, invented by Lieutenant Fiske and used by him when tied to the foremast of USS *Petral* during the battle of Manila Bay in 1898. These computers located in the Main Battery Plotting Room, below the armored deck, were coupled to two Mark 38 range-finding directors, one located atop the superstructure tower, with the other director located on the aft superstructure just forward of Turret 3. These fire-control computers were able to project the targets' future position, aim the guns for deflection, range, and time-of-shell flight, as well as incorporate a host of atmospheric and ballistic calculations, and allow for ship maneuver, pitch, roll, yaw, and speed. This mechanical/electrical machine performed a task equivalent to that of a quarterback, who uses inherent judgment and muscle-control of a quarterback when throwing a football from his own half to a point in space downfield to which a sprinting wide receiver will reach to catch the ball and score a touchdown.

USS *SOUTH DAKOTA*

This drawing of the *South Dakota* depicts her at the end of the Pacific war, bristling with 40mm Bofors and 20mm guns.

Built 47ft shorter at the waterline than *North Carolina*, the top-down view clearly shows the hull fairing out from the position of the first 16-inch gun turret.

The profile view readily captures the massive superstructure of bridge, conning tower, and tower with the incorporated funnel. This massive superstructure provided an ample aiming point during the night battle off Guadalcanal, and suffered 15 hits from IJN cruisers and destroyers. *South Dakota* gained a reputation as a jinxed ship: hitting an uncharted coral reef in the Tonga Islands, being hit by 500lb bombs at the battles of Santa Cruz and the Philippine Sea, and suffering the above damage off Guadalcanal, a collision with the destroyer USS *Mahan* and the explosion of a propellant case requiring the flooding of the magazine for turret two while rearming. However, *South Dakota* was credited with downing 31 Japanese aircraft, the largest number by any fast battleship.

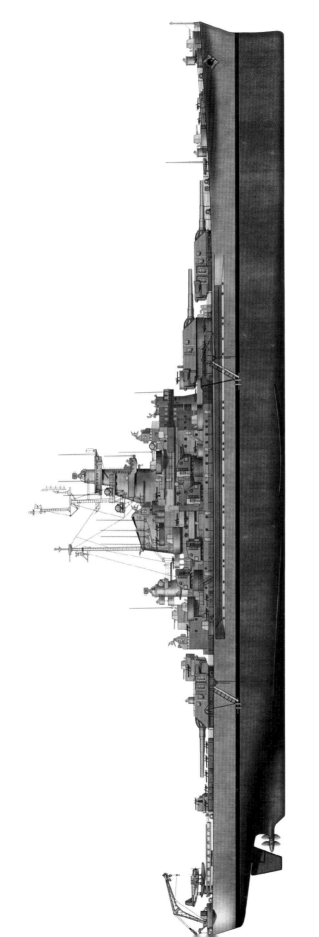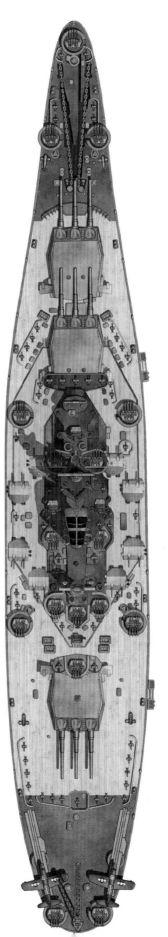

A 1.1-inch anti-aircraft gun as originally fitted to *North Carolina*. This gun was prone to jamming if not well maintained. Additionally the weight of bullets fired was insufficient to down an attacking aircraft within the time of the closing range. These guns were replaced by 40mm Bofors.

The CXAM-1 air-search radar antenna, referred to as the "bedspring," being fixed to the top of the foremast. Radar was a war-winning technology for the US Navy.

The secondary armament of dual-purpose 5-inch guns were controlled by four Mark 1 secondary battery computers, located in a separate plotting room. These computers were each coupled with one of the four Mark 37 directors, one forward, one aft, and one either side of the ship. The Mark 1 computer performed the same tasks as the Mark 38, and in addition performed these tasks more quickly for fast-moving targets and calculated altitude of the target in respect of aircraft.

Both plotting rooms also contained a large switchboard that allowed the function of each plot to be switched to its back-up plot located forward of Turret 3 in the event of the primary plot being inoperative. Two plots could also handle separate targets, linking separate directors to one or more gun turrets. Turret 2 also contained main battery plotting instruments to provide a further back up.

Radar

Both the North Carolina and South Dakota class battleships were designed before radar became an integral component of ship design. The *North Carolina* had an air-search CXAM radar installed on her foremast in August 1941. This radar was upgraded to a SK-2 set in March 1943, and in September 1944 upgraded with a SK-2 17ft dish antenna. Mark 3 fire-control radar was installed on top of both fore and aft Mark 38 directors and integrated into the main plot. The Mark 3 was a 40cm radar with a 12-degree beam to provide accurate range and bearing input. This radar was upgraded to a 10cm Mark 8 that scanned at ten scans per second and could range out to 40,000 yards.

Mark 4 fire-control radar, capable of detecting both surface and air targets, was installed only on three of the Mark 37 secondary directors. The aft Mark 37 director was left without a radar antenna, as the height of the intended antenna would have interfered with the Mark 3 radar on the aft Mark 38 director. The Mark 4 was upgraded to Mark 12 and fitted to all Mark 37 directors, as a higher mount had been installed on the Mark 38 director for its radar antenna.

Aircraft

Both the North Carolina and South Dakota class battleships each carried three aircraft, primarily for spotting the fall of shot from the main armament during long-range gunfire. The aircraft were also used for anti-submarine patrols, air-sea rescue, and communicating with shore stations.

Each aircraft, an OS2U Vought Sikorsky Kingfisher, was launched from one of two 68ft catapults located port and starboard at the stern of the ship. Two aircraft were stowed on the catapults with the third aircraft stowed on a dolly between the catapults. The Kingfisher was a single-float aircraft that would land on a slick of still

North Carolina in her commissioning light gray paint scheme.

water created by the battleship turning 90 degrees across the wind, then taxi up to the stern of the ship where a hook on the underside of the float would engage a rope sled towed by the ship; the aircraft crane could then reach out to hoist the Kingfisher back on board.

FAST BATTLESHIP OPERATIONS

The North Carolina and South Dakota class battleships were designed for classic line-of-battle conflict. Their high speed, relative to earlier battleships, enabled them to act as a fast wing of the US battle line, counter Japanese fast battleships, and dictate the pace and direction of battle to the enemy battle line. The operative war plans in late 1941, for both the Japanese and US navies, culminated in an Armageddon battleship battle somewhere in the western Pacific.

The naval war in the Atlantic and European waters between September 1939 and late 1941 had already shown the growing lethal capability of carrier-launched and land-based aircraft against warships. Of particular note, on the night of November 11, 1940, Swordfish aircraft from the carrier HMS *Illustrious* attacked the Italian battle fleet in Taranto harbor with torpedoes and bombs, and sank two battleships, damaging a third as well as two cruisers and two fleet auxiliaries. On March 28, 1941, an Albacore aircraft launched from HMS *Formidable* made the first successful air-launched torpedo attack on a battleship underway at sea, when it hit the Italian battleship *Vittorio Veneto*. A torpedo hit on the Italian heavy cruiser *Pola* on the same day led to the battle of Matapan. On May 26, 1941, a Swordfish aircraft launched from HMS *Ark Royal* torpedoed the *Bismarck* at dusk during an Atlantic gale. The hit on the *Bismarck*'s rudder resulted in her being sunk the following day. All these attacks occurred at a range from the carrier greater than the range of a battleship's guns. During May 1941, the German Air Force established air superiority around Crete, and inflicted by dive-bombing severe damage and losses to Royal Navy ships evacuating Allied personnel from the island.

The Japanese carrier air attack on December 7, 1941 with torpedoes and bombs on the US Fleet at Pearl Harbor, and the sinking of the Royal Navy fast battleship HMS *Prince of Wales* and the battlecruiser HMS *Repulse*, operating without air cover, on December 10, by air-launched torpedoes in the South China Sea, brought home

The main battery plotting room showing the Ford Instrument Range Keeper Mark 8, Model 9, calibrated for 16-inch 45 caliber main guns. The main battery fire-control switchboard is shown to the right rear of the picture.

The main battery plotting room manned for action stations. The men are wearing sound activated microphones and headsets to receive input from the main director and radar for input into the Range Keeper.

the vulnerability of battleships to air-launched torpedoes.

The Atlantic

At the declaration of war with Japan and Germany, only two US fast battleships, *North Carolina* and *Washington*, had been commissioned. These two ships were involved with their shakedown and training cruises along the US eastern seaboard. Captain Badger of *North Carolina* requested and received 40 additional 20mm anti-aircraft (AA) guns to bolster his ship's defenses in December 1941. The ships were held on the eastern seaboard to counter the threat of the *Tirpitz* conducting raids on Atlantic convoys. This also reflected the primary US war aim of defeating Germany first, before turning its military and industrial might on Japan.

Washington sailed to join the Royal Navy Home Fleet at Scapa Flow on March 26, 1942, to participate in protecting convoys to Murmansk, Russia. During one such convoy, on May 1, *Washington* was following astern of HMS *King George V*, which collided with an accompanying destroyer, HMS *Punjabi*, cutting her in two. This ship sank in the path of *Washington*, which sailed between the two halves as the depth charges on board *Punjabi* exploded beneath the hull of *Washington*. However, no hull damage occurred. On July 14, 1942, *Washington* left the Royal Navy Home Fleet to return to the US for overhaul prior to sailing to the Pacific.

USS *Massachusetts* was commissioned on May 12, 1942 and on October 28 joined the Western Naval Task force for the invasion of North Africa. US forces were directed to Morocco and the Atlantic port city of Casablanca to secure sea communications to the US. The Vichy French Navy had docked the uncompleted battleship *Jean Bart*, together with a cruiser, ten destroyers, and 11 submarines, in Casablanca. Four shore batteries and a French Army Senegalese battalion guarded the city.

Massachusetts had launched her Kingfisher aircraft at dawn on November 8, and at 6:51am the Kingfishers came under AA fire. Then French fighters attacked the Kingfishers, but were promptly shot down by *Massachusetts*'s 5-inch guns, though not before one Kingfisher was shot down. At 7:01am the El Hank shore battery opened fire on the *Massachusetts* and straddled the ship. At 7:04am *Massachusetts* opened fire on the *Jean Bart* at a range of 24,000 yards, and in so doing was the first US battleship to fire her main armament against an enemy ship since USS *Oregon* fired at the retreating Spanish Fleet at the battle of Santiago on July 3, 1898. Although *Jean Bart* had not been completed, her forward turret of four 15-inch guns was operative and she returned fire at 7:08am, bracketing *Massachusetts*.

Massachusetts had to rely on air spotting to target *Jean Bart*, as her fire-control radar failed as a result of concussive shock from her main guns. Optical range finding was not possible because the French laid down a smoke screen, which together with the smoke and fire from exploding shells obscured the target. In total, *Massachusetts* fired nine 16-inch salvoes and hit *Jean Bart* five times, putting her out of action. These hits represented a 6.17 percent accuracy rate against a stationary target using indirect fire spotted by aircraft. *Massachusetts* next engaged the destroyer *Fougeux*, which had escaped Casablanca harbor and was advancing to make a torpedo attack. *Massachusetts* fired at a range of 11 miles and hit *Fougeux*, which blew up and sank. During this engagement an 8-inch shell fired from the El Hank battery hit *Massachusetts* on her portside deck opposite Turret 2, which penetrated and exploded in a second deck compartment without causing any casualties or serious damage. *Massachusetts* also hit the light cruiser *Primauguet* and the docked destroyer *Le Milan*.

The handling space between the powder magazine and the powder handling room. The transfer hopper with the handle in the up-position receives powder bags from the magazine. The bags are passed through the opposite hopper into the powder handling room where they are hoisted to the gun.

On November 12, *Massachusetts* sailed for the US to prepare for service in the Pacific. It is noteworthy that at the time of the action off Casablanca, *Massachusetts* had been in operation for only six months, which included her shakedown cruise and crew training. Of her total complement of 2,400, 2,000 were new recruits to the navy.

USS *Alabama* was commissioned on August 16, 1942. On April 2, 1943, *Alabama* and *South Dakota* sailed to join the Royal Navy Home Fleet at Scapa Flow to create a diversion for the forthcoming invasion of Sicily. These two battleships guarded against the *Tirpitz* making a foray either into the Atlantic or to raid the Russian convoys. Once this objective was achieved the *Alabama* and *South Dakota* sailed for the US on August 1, 1943 to prepare for service in the Pacific.

The Pacific

The *North Carolina*, commissioned on April 9, 1941, arrived in Pearl Harbor on July 11, 1942, and was the first new major warship to reinforce the outnumbered and embattled US Pacific Fleet. Between the attack on Pearl Harbor and this date, US Navy offensive operations in the Pacific had centered on carriers, supported by cruisers and destroyers. The battles of Coral Sea and Midway had again demonstrated the greater range of aircraft over battleship guns. At Midway, the IJN had employed their carriers in a box formation, and positioned their fast battleships in column formation on the distant beam of the box, or of an individual carrier. In these positions the fast battleships had not been able to successfully defend the carriers, resulting in four being sunk by US Navy carrier-launched dive-bombers.

In 1922, Commander Nimitz was studying at the NWC, and writing a thesis on the battle of Jutland. A key element of this battle was the difficulties Admiral Jellicoe had faced in deploying the 24 battleships of the Grand Fleet from the square cruising formation into line of battle. In searching for an alternative formation using the gaming board, Commander MacFall of the NWC suggested creating a circular cruising formation, with battleships in the center and supporting forces arranged in concentric circles around the battleships. Deployment from this cruising circular formation to line of battle was considered to be quicker and less difficult than from the square formation.

In 1923, Commander Nimitz was appointed tactical officer on board the fleet flagship USS *California* and introduced the circular formation to the battle fleet. The subsequent integration of the US Navy's first carrier, USS *Langley*, into the formation established that the fleet could readily adapt to the changes in course required by the *Langley* when she launched and recovered aircraft. The circular formation fell out of practice until early 1942 when now Admiral Nimitz became commander in chief of the US Pacific Fleet.

While steaming from the US east coast to Pearl Harbor, the air defense officer of the *North Carolina*, Lieutenant Commander Kirkpatrick, developed the manual for air defense, detailing control and coordination of Sky Control, radar, directors, and the plot to multiple targets. Training for rapid loading of the 5-inch dual-purpose guns was critical, particularly during high-angle firing. Training with the practice loading equipment was a daily regime for 5-inch gun crews. Additionally, the issue of managing the "dead-time" between taking the 5-inch shell out of the fusing pot, which set the fuse time as determined by the fire-control computer, and loading and firing the gun, was key. Time would vary depending on the elevation of the gun, and the stamina and loading skill of the gun crew. A delay of greater than two seconds in this process would mean that the target would move beyond the point of detonation. Kirkpatrick's air-defense manual was distributed to the other fast battleships as they entered the Pacific.

Guadalcanal

The *North Carolina* was assigned to Admiral Fletcher's task force for the invasion of Guadalcanal. The sinking of four IJN carriers at Midway had blunted Japan's expansion and provided an opportunity for the US Navy to commence a major offensive operation. The capture of Guadalcanal would secure sea communications between the US and Australia, from which an Allied thrust through Papua New Guinea to the Philippines would be launched.

During the planning for the invasion, Marine Colonel Maas, assigned to Admiral Fletcher's staff on board the flagship *Saratoga*, prepared a planning

memorandum in accordance with NWC methodology entitled "Estimate of the Situation (as of 15 July 1942)." In the section entitled "Operations Plan" Maas proposed that *North Carolina* reinforce the carrier task force, which would provide distant cover to the fire-support and screening group and the US Marine invasion force. Maas expected that Japan would reinforce its Guadalcanal forces under cover of three carriers, two to four battleships, and possibly eight cruisers.

In evaluating Maas's recommendations, Admiral Fletcher sought the advice of Commander Glover, the executive officer of *Saratoga*, as to whether a battleship would add to the overall capability of a fast-carrier task force, given that previous battleships did not have the speed to keep up with the carriers. Glover confirmed Maas's recommendation with the statement, "She can be a great help close in with her tremendous AA power."

Ready for war. North Carolina at Norfolk, June 1942, prior to sailing to join the Pacific Fleet. The ship's three Kingfisher aircraft are visible on the stern.

The battle of the Eastern Solomons

Following the successful invasion of Guadalcanal on August 7, 1942, and the capture of the airfield, renamed Henderson Field, by US Marines, it became imperative to the IJN that Henderson Field be either recaptured or put out of operation by air attack and naval bombardment. Then the IJN carriers could engage US carriers without the threat of attack by US aircraft based on Guadalcanal. With Henderson Field out of action, US aircraft would not be able to interdict troop convoys seeking to reinforce Japanese Army troops on Guadalcanal.

After the invasion of Guadalcanal, Admiral Fletcher kept his carrier task force deployed to the south of the island, out of range from land-based aircraft, waiting for the IJN to try to reinforce its Guadalcanal forces. This occurred on August 24, when American scouting planes located Japanese forces. The ensuing battle of the Eastern Solomons saw Admiral Fletcher's carrier-launched aircraft sink the light carrier *Ryujo*. But the two large carriers, *Shokaku* and *Zuikaku*, survived the air attacks and were able to launch a massive air raid of approximately 80 aircraft against *Saratoga* and *Enterprise*.

The *North Carolina* was stationed 2,500 yards astern of *Enterprise* holding the rear position of the circle with *Enterprise* in the middle of the circle. Two cruisers, *Portland* and *Atlanta*, with six destroyers comprised the balance of the circular formation. The formation was steaming at 27 knots and *North Carolina* maintained this speed for over an hour, matching *Enterprise*'s radical course changes to avoid attack. However, during the air attack *Enterprise* increased speed to 30 knots and gradually pulled ahead

C

USS *NORTH CAROLINA*

This image of USS *North Carolina*, depicts her in March 1943, after she had the SK 2 air-search radar fitted.

North Carolina displays the innovative design features that contrast her with pre-1922 battleships. The 120 foot high superstructure tower replaced the tripod and cage masts of earlier ships and provided a more stable environment for main armament fire-control, as well as platforms for conning, sky control, battle lookouts, flag and signal lamp locations, and space for radio and radar antennas. Four propellers and twin rudders made the ship highly maneuverable, while the sweeping weather deck hull form, combined with the bulbous bow, made the ship very seaworthy. During the typhoon of December 18, 1944, *North Carolina* rolled, on average, only 10 degrees, with a maximum roll of 43 degrees.

The two main fire-control and four secondary directors were mounted to provide maximum elevation and fields of view. The secondary 5-inch armament mounted in revolving turrets located on and above the main weather deck had wide fields of fire and contrasted with the casement locations of secondary guns in pre-1922 battleships.

The ship was manned by 141 officers, 2,115 sailors, and 85 marines during wartime. The vast fuel and stores capacity of the ship enabled her to operate at sea for lengthy periods of time.

Image provided courtesy of Battleship *North Carolina*.

Key

1 Multiple 20mm gun mounts
2 Forward 16-inch gun turret with 50ft optical rangefinder
3 Armored conning tower
4 Pilothouse
5 Mark 37 5-inch gun director
6 Mark 4 fire-control radar
7 Stryker's bridge
8 Sky control
9 Mark 38 16-inch gun director with 26.5ft optical range finder
10 Mark 4 fire-control radar
11 SK 2 air-search radar
12 Port and starboard Mark 37 5-inch gun directors
13 Twin smoke stacks
14 Surface search radar
15 Aft Mark 38 16-inch gun director and Mark 4 radar
16 Aft Mark 37 5-inch gun director and Mark 4 radar

17 Vought Kingfisher float-plane – three carried
18 Float-plane crane
19 Aft 40mm gun mounts
20 Steering flat
21 Crew mess deck
22 40mm gun mount
23 Propeller shaft
24 Boiler in machinery room
25 5-inch gun mount and handling room
26 Combat information center
27 Admiral's quarters
28 Officer's wardroom

29 Gun plotting room
30 16-inch gun house
31 Armored barbette and shell flat
32 Powder magazine
33 Store rooms
34 Anchor chain lockers
35 Crew mess deck
36 Hull number
37 Port anchor

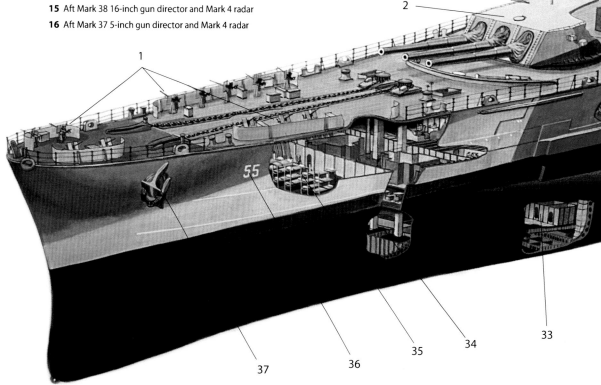

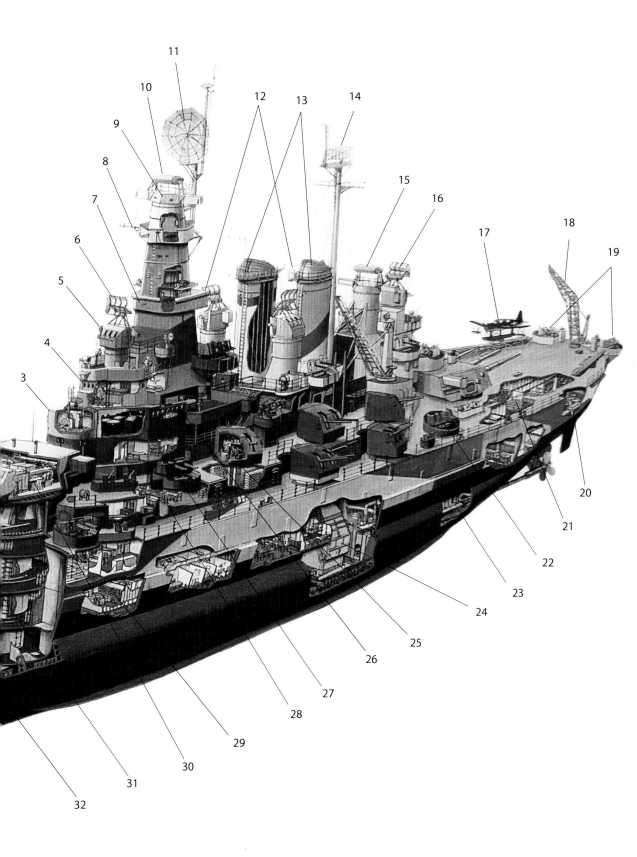

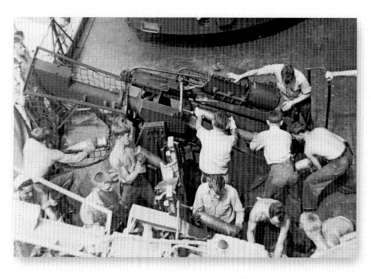
Practice, practice, practice. 5-inch gun crews use the practice loading machine to improve their loading drill and increase the critical rate of fire during air attack.

of *North Carolina* so that by the end of the action *North Carolina* was 4,000 yards behind *Enterprise*.

At 3:30pm local time, *North Carolina*'s CXAM radar registered Japanese aircraft at 70 miles distance. At 5:11pm dive-bombers were visually sighted and Sky-control took command of air defense. At 5:12pm *North Carolina* opened fire with Mounts 2, 4, and 6 portside 5-inch gun turrets at 15 dive-bombers attacking the *Enterprise*. The 5-inch shells were fused for 1.8 seconds and the volume of fire placed an umbrella of bursting shells over *Enterprise* and caused many of the dive-bombers to break from their attack.

At 5:13pm the *North Carolina* came under attack by ten dive-bombers attacking the starboard beam. Mounts 1, 3, and 5 starboard-side 5-inch gun turrets opened fire and turned away several of the bombers. Only three bombs were dropped and they all missed.

Next, torpedo and glide bombers attacked the ship from different directions and the full AA armament opened fire – 20 5-inch guns, 16 1.1-inch canons, 40 20mm, and 26 50-caliber machine-guns. The resultant volume of fire, with accompanying sheets of flame, tracers, and smoke from the guns, was such that Admiral Kinkaid on board *Enterprise* signaled "Are you on fire?" No one had seen a fast battleship fire all its guns in action before.

At 5:15pm a further dive-bombing attack was made by four aircraft on the port quarter with four bombs landing close to the port and starboard catapults, resulting in a volume of water coming on board that knocked the aft 20mm gunners down. *North Carolina* was not hit during the attacks, but one attacking aircraft strafed the ship with machine-gun fire and killed one sailor, a loader on an aft 20mm gun. During the action, *North Carolina* gun crews fired 841 5-inch shells, 1,067 1.1-inch shells, 7,425 20mm shells, and 8,641 50-caliber bullets. The decks around the 5-inch gun turrets were covered with shell casings, ejected from the 5-inch guns after being fired.

The attacks were over by 5:20pm and *North Carolina*, in what the crew described as "seven minutes of hell," was credited with destroying seven aircraft and possibly 14. But her more noteworthy action was in using her 5-inch guns to defend *Enterprise*, which was the main target of the attack. *Enterprise* suffered three bomb hits, but her damage-control crews were able to contain the damage and *Enterprise* was able to recover aircraft and continue at full speed.

Having failed to sink the two US carriers, and having lost one carrier and 42 aircraft shot down by US carrier aircraft and AA fire, the IJN forces withdrew. The planned reinforcement of Guadalcanal with a troop convoy sailing without air cover was stopped and

US formation of the battle of the Eastern Solomons.

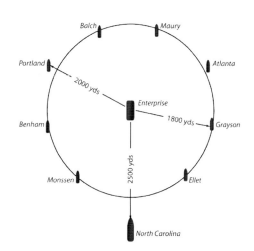

devastated on August 25 by US Marine and Navy aircraft flying from Henderson Field.

The battle of the Eastern Solomons was a critical strategic success for the US Navy, and another major carrier victory for Admiral Fletcher, along with Coral Sea and Midway. While stopping Japan reinforcing its troops on Guadalcanal and inflicting on it a further carrier loss and the destruction of naval aircraft and crews, the actions of *North Carolina* in the battle established a new role for fast battleships as close-in AA escorts to fast carriers. Additionally, the battleship's traditional role of providing big-gun firepower was seen as critical during nighttime when carriers were vulnerable to surface ships.

Mark 1 Eyeballs supplement radar to spot incoming aircraft.

After the battle Admiral Kinkaid signaled Admiral Nimitz in Pearl Harbor, "The presence of a fast battleship in Task Force 16 ... during action on 24 August was a distinct asset because of her demonstrated fire power against attacking aircraft and her inherent strength against possible surface contacts. ... the station of the *North Carolina* in cruising disposition and particularly in tight screening dispositions during air attacks should be downwind from carrier as was the case on 24 Aug with thoroughly satisfactory results."

The combination of mutually supporting fast carrier and fast battleship in a task force created for the US Navy an unbeatable weapon system. No carrier escorted by a fast battleship was lost to air attack, and no fast battleship was lost during the remainder of the war.

The unique and first-time role *North Carolina* played in the battle was reflected in Captain Fort's After Action report for the ship. Notwithstanding that his was the latest and most powerful battleship in the US Fleet, Captain Fort wrote in his opening paragraphs that "The *North Carolina* was operating with Task Force 16 as a cruiser." This statement indicates that at the time of his writing, the US Navy had yet to formulate a role for the new fast battleships working with fast carriers. In the absence of a formalized role, operational necessity, as determined by the admirals on the spot, Fletcher and Kinkaid, resulted in fast battleships being used as close-in AA escorts to fast carriers.

Baptism of fire. Battle of the Eastern Solomons. *Enterprise* taken from the yardarm of *North Carolina* under air attack, but protected by an anti-aircraft umbrella. Note the row of splashes from a 20mm gun between the ships.

For *North Carolina*, four elements of the battle proved unsatisfactory:

- 1.1-inch cannon
  The 1.1-inch cannon did not deliver sufficient weight of shells to down an aircraft during its attack mode. Kirkpatrick noted that this gun was liable to break down due to weak recoil and ejection systems. These guns were subsequently replaced with four-barrel 40mm Bofors guns.
- Conning during air-attack
  The executive officer, Commander Stryker, conned the ship during the air attack from a secondary conning position located at level seven, mid-way up the superstructure

A Japanese plane splashes astern of USS *Enterprise* during the battle.

tower. Visibility was severely limited through battle-slits cut into the skin of the tower. Stryker subsequently had a walkway built around the outside of the tower at the secondary conning level, so that he had unrestricted visibility in future battles.

- Sky Control and radar overwhelmed
  Sky Control, directors, and the radar system missed locating a number of heavy bombers at 15,000ft that attacked *North Carolina* at the same time as the torpedo and glide bombers. Fortunately the released bombs fell between *North Carolina* and *Enterprise*.

- Sea impact on bow gunners
  Sailing at full speed resulted in significant spray and water coming over the forecastle and adversely impacting the forward 20mm gunners.

Torpedo attack

On September 15, 1942, the IJN submarine I-19, on picket patrol south of the Solomon Islands, fired six Type 95 torpedoes at the carrier USS *Wasp*. Three torpedoes struck the *Wasp*, which eventually sank. Two of the three torpedoes that missed the *Wasp* continued their run, with one hitting the destroyer USS *O'Brien* and blowing off her bow. The other torpedo struck *North Carolina* on her port side adjacent to Turret 1 at 2:52pm, killing five sailors and wounding 23. The 891lb warhead in the torpedo blasted a hole

"SEVEN MINUTES OF HELL"

This picture captures the moment when the *North Carolina* opened fire with all her AA guns to ward off a simultaneous and coordinated attack by Japanese dive-bombers and torpedo planes. At the same time, *North Carolina* is firing her 5-inch guns at Japanese aircraft attacking *Enterprise* by placing an umbrella of exploding shells over this ship, which the attacking aircraft have to penetrate in order to release their bombs. Until this moment, no one had witnessed the amount of AA gunfire a fast battleship could produce. Admiral Kinkaid on board the *Enterprise* signaled *North Carolina*, "Are you on fire?" A Japanese aircraft, after releasing its bomb, flew alongside *North Carolina* for the first view of this new US battleship.

North Carolina is following astern of *Enterprise*, and both ships are twisting and turning to avoid falling bombs and torpedoes. *Enterprise* has increased speed to her maximum 33 knots, but *North Carolina* can only manage 27 knots and will eventually fall behind *Enterprise* by two miles; however the range of her 5-inch guns still protects the *Enterprise*.

The AA performance of *North Carolina* in the battle of the Eastern Solomons, notwithstanding her lack of the new 40mm Bofors gun, led to the new role for fast battleships as close-in AA escorts for carriers, and no US carrier escorted by a fast battleship was sunk by air attack for the rest of the war.

Empty shell casings litter the deck from a 5-inch gun mount, with the practice loading machines in the background.

32ft long and 18ft high in the hull, 20ft below the waterline. The first torpedo bulkhead between frames 46 and 50 was demolished and the next two torpedo bulkheads were forced inboard with 1,000 tons of water taken on board creating a 5-degree list to port. This list was corrected within five minutes by counter-flooding on the starboard side. Flooding water reached the handling room for Turret 1 and burning oil from ruptured oil tanks entered the forward magazine, but the activated sprinkler system extinguished the flames. *North Carolina* was able to increase speed to 25 knots and maintain her position screening the carrier USS *Hornet*. The shock from the explosion put the search radar at the top of the foremast out of action.

Following temporary repairs at Tongatabu in the Tonga Islands by the repair ship USS *Vestal*, *North Carolina* sailed to Pearl Harbor, where she arrived on September 30 and stayed until November 17, 1942 for permanent repairs. While in Pearl Harbor the 1.1-inch canons were removed and replaced by 15 mounts of four-barrel 40mm Bofors guns. The walkway around level seven of the superstructure tower was also constructed, and thereafter referred to as "Stryker's Bridge." This walkway was unique to *North Carolina* and helped identify the ship from her otherwise twin, *Washington*.

South Pacific reinforcements

On September 4, 1942, *South Dakota* arrived in Tonga after her commissioning on March 20, 1942. On September 6 she hit an uncharted coral reef and damaged her hull bottom. The repair ship *Vestal* had her divers check the ship's hull and seams. The divers reported the damage as a series of splits extending 150ft along the ship's bottom. By September 8, *Vestal*'s repairmen, together with men of the battleship's crew, managed to mend the damage sufficiently to allow the ship to leave for Pearl Harbor for permanent repairs. *South Dakota* returned to the South Pacific on October 24 as part of Task Force 16, escorting *Enterprise*, which had also been repaired at Pearl Harbor from the damage incurred in the battle of the Eastern Solomons.

On September 14, *Washington* arrived in Tonga, after her commissioning on May 15, 1941, and Admiral Willis "Ching" Lee joined the ship as

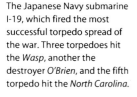

The Japanese Navy submarine I-19, which fired the most successful torpedo spread of the war. Three torpedoes hit the *Wasp*, another the destroyer *O'Brien*, and the fifth torpedo hit the *North Carolina*.

commander, Battleship Division 6. US naval forces continued to cover troop and supply convoys to Guadalcanal from New Caledonia.

Anticipating a further major attempt by Japan to reinforce its troops and recapture Guadalcanal, on October 23, *Washington*, three cruisers, and six destroyers were ordered to patrol south of Guadalcanal to cover the "slot." *Enterprise*, *South Dakota*, *Hornet*, and accompanying cruisers were to sail towards the Santa Cruz Islands located to the east of Guadalcanal to prevent any Japanese forces moving south on the Pacific side of the Solomon Islands chain.

Battle of Santa Cruz

The battle of Santa Cruz took place on October 26, 1942. The IJN Combined Fleet was organized with the three carriers, *Shokaku*, *Zuikaku*, and the light carrier *Zuiho* as the Carrier Striking Force. A Vanguard Group of two fast battleships, *Hiei* and *Kirishima*, and three cruisers preceded the carriers and was intended to provide a target for attacking US carrier aircraft and thereby blunt any attack on the following carriers. Additionally, the Vanguard Group was to hunt down the US carrier force once located and slowed by attacks from the carriers. An Advance Group of five cruisers with two fast battleships, *Kongo* and *Haruna*, and the carrier *Junyo* was to attack Henderson Field.

I-19's torpedo caused a hole 32ft long and 18ft in depth in *North Carolina*'s port side adjacent to the forward main gun turret.

Once scouting forces from both sides had located each other's main carrier forces, air attacks were launched, which passed each other in mid-air on their way to their respective targets. *Hornet* and her four accompanying cruisers were operating ten miles from *Enterprise*, *South Dakota*, and two cruisers. A line of tropical squalls covered *Enterprise* and her escorts. The first air attack of 36 torpedo and dive-bombers focused on the *Hornet* at 10:09am; she suffered two torpedo hits on her starboard side and three bomb hits by 10:14am, had to be subsequently abandoned, and eventually sank.

The next wave of attack comprising 20 dive-bombers commenced at 11:12am on the stern of the *Enterprise*. *South Dakota* was stationed 1,000 yards off *Enterprise*'s starboard side and opened fire. The second attack comprised both torpedo and dive-bombers, which approached from different directions and were well coordinated to create multiple attacking points. This attack lasted until 11:52am. The *Enterprise* was hit by two bombs during the attack, but was still able to steam and operate aircraft. *Enterprise* also landed a large number of *Hornet*'s aircraft, as that carrier slowly succumbed to the damage she had sustained, and found herself with her flight deck inoperative.

At 12:19pm a further wave of 24 torpedo and dive-bombers attacked from off *South Dakota*'s port bow, using the low cloud of the squall line to hide their approach. At 12:29pm a dive-bomber appeared from a 1,000ft cloud base on the port bow and scored a hit on *South Dakota*'s number one 16-inch gun turret with a 500lb bomb. While this turret remained operative, the bomb damaged two 16-inch gun barrels of Turret 2, which was trained over Turret 1. Shrapnel from the exploding bomb killed one sailor and wounded 49 others, including Captain Gatch. The captain had left his position inside the heavily armored conning tower with its limited visibility to improve his view of the attacking aircraft, and had stationed himself on the open catwalk outside the conning tower, above and behind Turret 2.

I-19's torpedo also buckled the revolving deck within *North Carolina*'s powder handling room.

The *Enterprise* and *South Dakota* were the only ships armed with the new 40mm Bofors gun. The shells from this gun were heavier than shells from the 1.1-inch canon and far more effective against attacking aircraft. The 40mm shells were fused to explode at 4,000ft, providing a curtain of exploding shells through which attacking aircraft had to penetrate. Additionally, ships in the *Enterprise* group carried in total 108 20mm guns versus 52 in the *Hornet*'s group. The high rate of fire from these 20mm guns was particularly effective against low-flying aircraft and accounted for the majority of the 26 aircraft that *South Dakota* claimed.

Aircraft from *Hornet* severely damaged *Shokaku* and the cruiser *Chikuma*, and aircraft from *Enterprise* bombed *Zuiho*. Both of these Japanese carriers required extensive repairs in Japan as a result of this battle. As important, Japan lost 99 aircraft and 145 aircrew from its small population of battle-trained airmen.

South Dakota entered the battle only seven months after her commissioning. Her crew contained a large percentage of men new to the navy and who manned the 20mm guns on the ship's exposed decks. This new crew and the crews of the other ships were exposed to unrelenting air attacks as a result of misdirection to *Enterprise*'s combat air patrol by fighter-direction officers that allowed Japanese aircraft to attack unopposed by defending fighters. Therefore the AA guns of *Enterprise*, *South Dakota*, and the two cruisers became the primary defense against attacking aircraft.

Naval battles of Guadalcanal

The successful battles of the Eastern Solomons and Santa Cruz, together with aircraft from Henderson Field, gave the US Navy and Marines control of the air over and around Guadalcanal and up the slot during the day. The US Navy was therefore able to supply and reinforce the Marines fighting on Guadalcanal, and in particular defending Henderson Field against Japanese troops. However, during the night when aircraft could not operate, the IJN was able to land troops and resupply its existing troops on the island, and

16-INCH GUN TURRET

The 16-inch gun had a range of 36,900 yards, a muzzle velocity of 2,300 feet per second, and could fire two types of shell: a 2,700lb armor-piercing shell capable of penetrating 20 inches of armor at a range of 15,000 yards, for use against armored ships or fortified emplacements, or a 1,900lb high-capacity shell for use against unarmored ships or soft land targets.

The magazine, storing the powder charges, was positioned on the lower two levels of the ship. The charges were stored in canisters, stacked in racks. When needed, they were removed from their canisters, moved along a conveyor to a powder scuttle, and passed through to the powder handling room. Here, six charges would be loaded into an electric hoist and raised to the gun house to either the left or the right of the gun breech. Above the powder handling room, two decks – the projectile rings – stored the 16-inch shells. Shells were loaded into a hoist which lifted them up an enclosed tube to the gun house, where it would exit the hoist to the rear of the gun. The end of the tube hoist comprised a tilting tray that moved the shell from the vertical to a 5-degree horizontal loading position, and formed a loading tray to span the space between the hoist and the gun breech. A rammer would then push the shell into the breech. The door to the powder hoist would then be opened towards the loading tray, creating a shelf for the charges to slide into the loading tray, from where they would then be slowly rammed into the breech. After inserting a firing pin, the breech was closed and the gun fired.

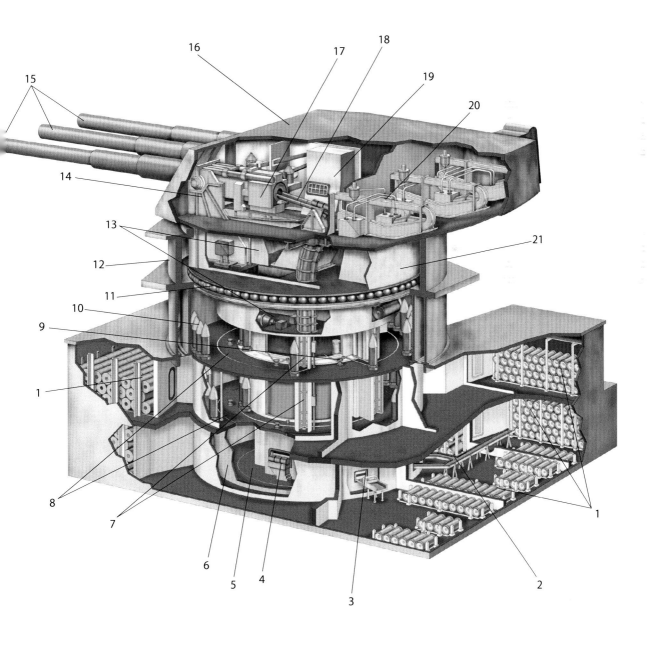

then bombard Henderson Field. The US Marines named this nightly bombardment "The Tokyo Express."

The US Navy had cruisers, destroyers, and Motor Torpedo Boats (MTBs) standing guard on the seaward side of Henderson Field in Savo Sound, between Guadalcanal and Florida Islands. However, only a few of the larger ships had radar, and experience in its use was limited. Additionally, the northern sea approach to Guadalcanal was bisected by Savo Island and also guarded. The IJN had trained vigorously for night battle, including the launching of "Long Lance" torpedoes before firing their guns to achieve maximum surprise. In a series of night battles, Savo Island, Lunga Point, Cape Esperance, and the first battle of Guadalcanal, the IJN sank four US cruisers, one Australian cruiser, and seven destroyers. In these battles the IJN lost one cruiser and four destroyers. In addition, the IJN bombarded Henderson Field on a regular nightly basis. However, despite the nightly bombardment, Henderson Field remained operative and on November 14, 1942 Marine and Navy aircraft sank a heavy cruiser and the fast battleship *Hiei*, both of which had been severely damaged by US cruisers during the first battle of Guadalcanal, as well as six troop transports.

Following these naval losses, and anticipating further bombardment of Henderson Field, Admiral Halsey, who had replaced Admiral Ghormley as commander South Pacific Forces, ordered Admiral Lee to position his flagship *Washington* and the *South Dakota* plus four destroyers to the north of Savo Island to intercept any IJN forces steaming south to Savo Sound. This was a high-risk operation for these new high-value battleships, as the waters around Savo Sound were not well charted, with the potential for a large ship to hit unknown coral reefs. The waters were also narrow for large ships, and without sufficient maneuvering room they were vulnerable to torpedo attacks. Additionally, the battleships and destroyers were a scratch force, having never operated together before.

As night approached on November 14, 1942, Admiral Lee moved his task force north of Guadalcanal and eastwards to the northeast of Savo Island. The four destroyers in line ahead preceded *Washington*, with *South Dakota* astern. A US submarine, *Trout*, on patrol up the slot radioed that she had spotted large enemy units moving south. This comprised a bombardment

Dauntless dive-bombers circle over the *North Carolina* in March 1944 as the ship sails towards Emirau Island.

The *North Carolina* passing astern of a US carrier.

group, centered on the fast battleship *Kirishima*, four cruisers, and nine destroyers, followed by a convoy of troop transports.

Admiral Lee turned his force south to move into Savo Sound. At this point Lee heard over the tactical voice radio talk between patrolling MTBs that they had spotted Lee's task force but did not know if it was Japanese or US. Admiral Lee used the "talk between ships" radio to talk to the MTBs using his Naval Academy nickname "Ching" for identification, saying, "This is Ching Chong China Lee. Refer your big boss about Ching Lee. Call off your boys!" With identity established, Admiral Lee then circumnavigated Savo Island, finally heading northwest between Savo Island on his starboard bow and the northern tip of Guadalcanal named Cape Esperance on his port bow. In addition to his colorful nickname, Admiral Lee was an expert on radar and gunnery, and this would be a major factor in the action about to unfold.

At 00:01am on November 15, *Washington*'s radar located Japanese ships to the east of Savo Island at a range of 18,500 yards. With the aid of moonlight, visibility was approximately nine miles. At 00:16am *Washington* opened fire with *South Dakota* following one minute later. This represented the first time a battle line formation of US battleships opened fire on enemy ships. The fire from *Washington* totaled 42 16-inch shells and was held until 00:19am. The target was the cruiser *Sendai*, which laid down a smoke screen and quickly retired without damage. Both battleships fired their 5-inch secondary batteries at Japanese destroyers at a range of 15,000 yards.

At 00:20am Lee's four destroyers opened fire on Japanese ships approaching from the northwest side of Savo Island. Within 20 minutes, two destroyers, USS *Walke* and *Preston*, were blazing wrecks and sinking, with the other two, USS *Gwin* and *Benham*, badly damaged and retiring from action.

20mm gun crews at the ready.

During this same 20-minute period, *Washington* and *South Dakota* fired both main and secondary armaments intermittently at targets appearing from around Savo Island to their northeast. The destroyer *Ayanami* was hit with two 5-inch shells from *South Dakota* later in the night.

At 00:33am the concussive shock from firing all bearing guns caused an electrical

short circuit on *South Dakota*, which tripped a circuit breaker incorrectly connected to the ship's electrical system. Her radar, fire-control circuits, turret motors, ammunition hoists, and radios became inoperative until power was restored at 00:36am. At this time, *South Dakota* veered to her starboard to avoid the blazing wrecks of *Walke* and *Preston* and was subsequently silhouetted when passing them, providing enemy forces with an illuminated target. *Washington* ahead of *South Dakota* had turned to port keeping the wrecks on her engaged side and so remained invisible to the Japanese.

At 00:42am, *South Dakota*'s Turret 3 firing over her stern set fire to her two Kingfisher aircraft. The next salvo from this turret then blew the two aircraft overboard and dampened the fires. *South Dakota* was now visible to the Japanese, who then turned on their searchlights, focusing on her superstructure. *South Dakota* became their primary target at 00:48am and suffered a hail of fire of 26 hits, with 15 of these on her bridge and superstructure. Fourteen of these hits were by 8-inch shells and one by a 5-inch shell. Turret 3 was hit by a 14-inch shell fired by the battleship *Kirishima* that detonated against the turret barbette but did not penetrate the armor. This hit locked the turret in place and did extensive damage to the deck. The integrity of the ship was not damaged, but her command and control were severely weakened both by casualties amongst officers and crew, and by damage to radar, fire-control circuits, and communication equipment. *South Dakota*, now ineffective as a fighting unit and unable to locate the position of *Washington*, withdrew from the battle, leaving *Washington* to face the Japanese fleet alone.

At 00:58am, the moon set and visibility dropped from nine miles to less than three within minutes. *Washington* had been firing her 5-inch guns at the

NIGHT BATTLE OFF GUADALCANAL

This picture depicts the *Washington* at 01:02am on November 15, 1942, when she is firing her third salvo of 16-inch guns at the IJN fast battleship *Kirishima*. The opening salvos, fired at a range of 8,400 yards, have started a fire amidships on board *Kirishima* in its starboard secondary casements. *Kirishima* is illuminated by multiple star shells fired by the starboard stern 5-inch gun turret on board *Washington*.

Washington and *Kirishima* are approaching each other with a combined speed of 54 knots, rather than on parallel courses in the classic battleship duel tactic. This approach and the high speed means that the change of rate is high and the amount of lead-off for deflection is also high, rather than the constant bearing that a parallel course would create. In the first two minutes and 29 seconds *Washington* fires 39 16-inch shells at *Kirishima*. Then *Washington* ceases fire for 90 seconds, as reports advise the target is sunk. However, when *Kirishima* opens fire on *Washington*, the latter returns fire for another three minutes and sends 36 16-inch shells towards *Kirishima*, which then ceases fire and turns to port. *Washington* ceases fire, aware that *South Dakota* is somewhere astern and off her starboard quarter, and Admiral Lee assumes she is nearing the same bearing as *Kirishima*.

To the right of the picture is *South Dakota*, which has been illuminated by searchlights from the IJN cruisers *Atago* and *Takao* and is being heavily hit by these ships as well as *Kirishima*. *South Dakota* is hit 26 times by Japanese shells. Although her armor belt is not penetrated, and the ship is able to steam and maneuver, her fighting capability has been rendered inoperative through damage to the command and control officers, crew, and equipment located in the bridge and superstructure tower. *South Dakota* withdraws from the battle.

Kirishima sinks in the early hours, as her crew is unable to control the flooding caused by the hits from *Washington*.

Admiral Lee and *Washington* achieved a major victory over the IJN, which was unable to bombard Henderson Field or protect the troop transports bringing reinforcements and supplies, which were destroyed in the morning by US aircraft flying from Henderson Field. However, the uncertainty of not knowing where *South Dakota* was located relative to his position made Admiral Lee cautious when considering future night surface battles.

20mm gunners on the *North Carolina's* forecastle during an air attack off Okinawa, April 1945.

Japanese searchlights and had located the battleship *Kirishima* by the size of her radar return. At 01:00am *Washington* opened fire on *Kirishima* with her main armament. *Washington* and *Kirishima* were on nearly opposite courses. *Washington* was steering northwest, 290 degrees at 26 knots, and *Kirishima* steering southeast, 130 degrees at approximately 28 knots, a passing speed of 54 knots at a distance of 4,800 yards.

Between 01:00am and 01:02 and 39 seconds, *Washington* fired 39 rounds of 16-inch shells. *Washington* ceased fire for one and a half minutes, and then at 01:04 recommenced for a further three minutes during which she fired 36 rounds of 16-inch shells at *Kirishima*. As important, the turrets were training 20 degrees per minute, from 008 degrees to 148 degrees, in order to stay on target, when the forward turrets hit their stops at 01:07am and *Washington* ceased fire.

Two mounts of *Washington's* starboard 5-inch guns had also fired at *Kirishima* and two mounts fired at the ships firing on *South Dakota*. The fifth 5-inch mount fired 62 rounds of 5-inch star shells over *Kirishima*.

At 01:05am *Kirishima* turned to port and presented her stern and then port side to *Washington* and was hit on or near her rudder, jamming it. Two minutes later she began steering two complete circles before coming to a stop and sinking several hours later.

As *Kirishima* steamed past *Washington*, Admiral Lee was aware that *South Dakota* was nearing the same bearing as *Kirishima* and her two escorting cruisers. The danger of firing on *South Dakota* made Lee reluctant to maneuver to continue fire.

Washington claimed nine hits from 75 rounds of 16-inch shells fired, an accuracy rate of 12 percent against a target moving on a nearly opposite course with a high rate of deflection needed to account for the passing speed of 54 knots. Additionally, range and bearing were determined by radar. This result attests to the quality of the Ford Instrument Range Keeper, able to accurately determine firing solutions with a rapidly changing bearing and a course correction. US battleship radar negated Japanese night training. Research after the war, including interviews with surviving officers of *Kirishima*, suggests that *Kirishima* suffered 20 hits

South Dakota class battleship under air attack.

by 16-inch shells, as many shells falling short but continuing underwater to hit *Kirishima*'s hull. Should this be accurate, *Washington*'s accuracy rate was nearly 27 percent.

As a result of the battle, the bombardment of Henderson Field was cancelled. The troop transports following the Japanese bombardment force continued to Guadalcanal but were caught in daylight by aircraft from Henderson Field and destroyed. Only 2,000 troops survived to reach their colleagues on shore, but without their supplies of food and ammunition.

This battle, won by *Washington*, together with the success of the US Marines in defending Henderson Field, and the devastation of Japanese troop reinforcements by Marine and Navy aircraft, marked the beginning of the US drive toward defeating Japan.

November 1943 saw US forces in control of the Solomon Islands chain. Following *Washington*'s victory over the IJN in November 1942, this ship together with *North Carolina*, *Indiana*, and *Massachusetts* provided protection to the carriers *Saratoga* and HMS *Victorious* in support of the naval and Marine forces fighting their way up the Solomons. HMS *Victorious* was allocated to the South Pacific force while *Enterprise* was having her battle damage repaired.

Central Pacific offensive

On May 30, 1943, USS *Essex* arrived in Pearl Harbor, the first of the new fast carriers. Over the next few months, seven other new fast carriers joined *Essex*, demonstrating the output of America's vast industrial, shipbuilding, and military capability now geared to war. This force, named the Fifth Fleet, together with the Fifth Amphibious Force, six new fast battleships, *North Carolina*, *Washington*, *South Dakota*, *Massachusetts*, *Alabama* and *Indiana*, and four old battleships, was to spearhead the next phase of the Pacific war – the drive across the central Pacific – with the Gilbert Islands the first objective. Admiral Spruance, chief of staff to Admiral Nimitz, was appointed to command the Fifth Fleet.

Operation	Date	North Carolina	Washington	South Dakota	Indiana	Massachusetts	Alabama
Gilberts	11/43	√	√	√	√	√	√
Naru	12/43	√	√	√	√	√	√
Kwajalein	1/44	√	√	√	√	√	√
Truk	2/44	√	X	X	√	√	√
Palau	3/44	√	√	√	X	√	√
Hollandia	4/44	√	X	√	X	√	√
Marianas	6/44	√	√	√	√	X	√
Leyte	11/44	√	√	X	X	√	√
Luzon/China	1/45	√	√	√	X	√	X
Iwo Jima	2/45	√	√	√	√	√	X
Okinawa	3/45	√	√	√	√	X	√
Kyushu	7/45	√	√	√	√	√	√
Japan	8/45	√	X	√	√	√	√

X The ship did not participate in the operation as she was undergoing repair or refit.

Between November 1943 and August 1945, these six fast battleships took part in the following operations:

The majority of these operations involved multiple actions, from providing AA protection to the carriers to bombarding islands to be invaded by the Marines and Army.

Underpinning these operations were five critical technological or organizational developments:

- Proximity Fuse

  The Radio Proximity Fuse emitted radio waves from the shell in flight. When the waves hit a solid object within a 70-yard radius it detonated the shell. Used against aircraft this new proximity fuse significantly increased the chance of downing the aircraft. First used in action on January 1, 1943 by USS *Helena*, proximity fused 5-inch shells were available to the Fifth Fleet for the Gilberts operation.

- Radar

  Radar had been significantly enhanced and installed across the fleet, and this allowed task forces to maneuver at night and in bad weather with precision. As important, radar could now locate and track low-flying enemy aircraft.

- Fighter direction

  Formalizing radar and VHF communications into an air plot enabled fighter direction operations based upon a standard process, and allowed trained fighter direction officers to be established in all carriers. The RAF fighter direction methods used during the Battle of Britain in 1940 had been adapted and developed by Royal Navy carriers in 1940–41 during operations off Norway and in the Mediterranean. During the assignment of HMS *Victorious* with the US Navy, operating with *Saratoga* in the South Pacific, and her subsequent refitting in the Norfolk Navy Yard, her fighter direction organization, operating procedures, and the new vertical plot were inspected and then adopted by the US Navy, through Admiral King's Washington office.

- The Hellcat

  A new naval fighter aircraft, the Hellcat, specifically designed to beat the Zero, had been introduced to the Fleet.

- Circular formation

  The circular formation was perfected and applied to both task force formation and multiple task force formations. This resulted in multiple

G **CAMOUFLAGE SCHEMES 1941–43**

North Carolina had several camouflage schemes during her operational life. The objectives of camouflage were to reduce the visibility of the ship and to create confusion in the eyes of the viewer as to identity, heading, and speed of the ship. Naturally, this varied greatly, depending on the operational requirements. All paints used were matt to minimize the risk of reflection.

1. *North Carolina's* original camouflage scheme was the Measure 2 graded system applied in 1941. This consisted of ocean gray on the hull, haze gray on the superstructure, pale gray on top of the director tower, and deck blue on all decks.

2. The Measure 32 medium pattern system adopted in 1944 was easily the most dramatic of the North Carolina's history. Pale gray, haze gray, and navy blue were applied in polygonal patterns to confuse identity and heading, especially for observing submarines. This pattern was applied to most surface ships serving in the Pacific in 1944–45. Decks and horizontal surfaces remained deck blue.

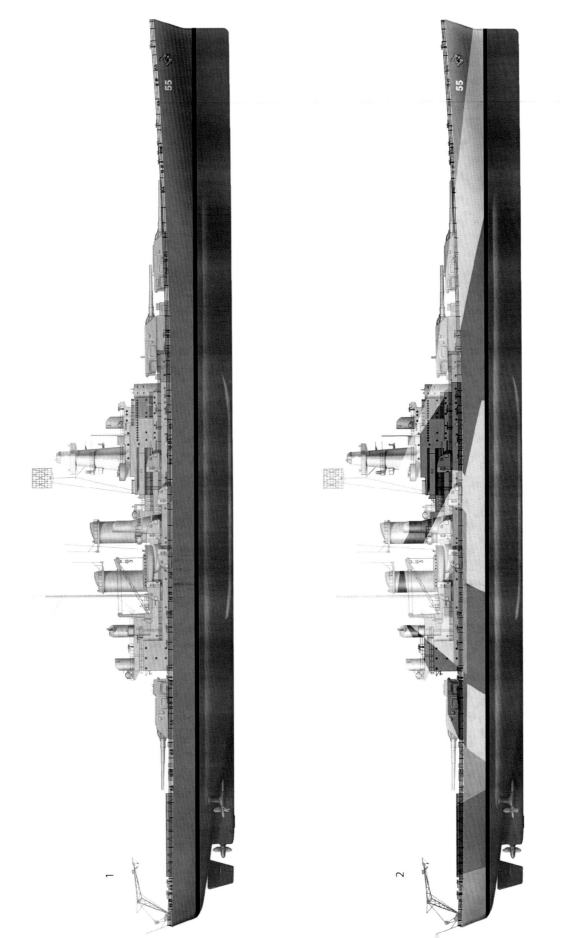

The *North Carolina* as seen from the fantail of *Washington*.

overlapping AA fields of fire. As the number of carriers increased, the formation had the carriers in the center surrounded by concentric circles of escorting ships, with fast battleships stationed in the first circle close in to the carriers. In the event that the Japanese battleship fleet came forward for battle, Admiral Spruance gave Admiral Lee, in command of the fast battleships, permission to form the classic line of battle formation outside the circular formation, with the carriers in the rear to provide air cover.

The battle of the Philippine Sea

As the US Navy advanced across the Pacific, with the US Marines storming and capturing, at heavy cost, Japanese Islands, the rate of attrition of Japanese aircraft and crews continued at a fearful pace. When the US invaded the Marianas, to acquire the airfields on Saipan, Tinian, and Guam, the Japanese Navy decided to commit its Mobile Fleet of nine remaining carriers to attack the US Fifth Fleet.

In organizing the fleet, Admiral Spruance had Admiral Lee withdraw his fast battleships, including two of the new Iowa class, from their AA escort positions to form his fast battleship circular steaming formation in preparation for deploying into line of battle. Lee's battleship force was positioned 15 miles ahead of the 15 carriers in four separate circular carrier formations. Lee headed westward to locate and destroy the Japanese Mobile Fleet. Lee was asked by Admiral Mitscher, commander of the carriers, "Do you desire night engagement?" Mitscher planned a strike by his carrier aircraft during the afternoon of June 18, 1944, with Lee engaging in a surface action after the air strike. Lee signaled Mitscher in reply, "Do not (repeat not) believe we should seek night engagement. Possible advantages of radar more than offset by difficulties of communication and lack of training in fleet tactics at night. Would press pursuit of damaged or fleeing enemy, however, at any time." Lee's experience in the night battle of Guadalcanal had shown him that notwithstanding having radar and talk between ship radios, confusion could and would easily arise with deadly effect. The prolonged role as escorts to the carriers had left no time for Lee to exercise his fast battleships in night battle. This decision by Lee negated one of the two real opportunities for fast battleships to engage IJN battleships in combat. The other opportunity was to come at Leyte Gulf.

Coming towards the battleships on the morning of June 19 was an air raid of 202 aircraft representing the first wave of Japanese carrier aircraft. This raid was larger than the 183 aircraft in the first wave of

US formation at the battle of the Philippine Sea.

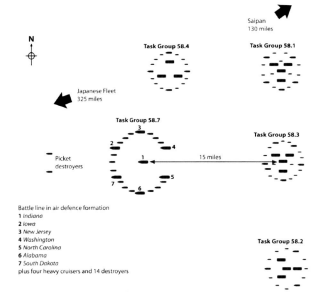

Battle line in air defence formation
1 *Indiana*
2 *Iowa*
3 *New Jersey*
4 *Washington*
5 *North Carolina*
6 *Alabama*
7 *South Dakota*
plus four heavy cruisers and 14 destroyers

A Japanese Betty bomber about to splash.

Japanese planes that attacked Pearl Harbor. *Alabama* was the first ship to locate the aircraft on her radar at a range of 140 miles at 9:57am. At 10:19am the order was given to the carriers to launch their Combat Air Patrols (CAP), and 220 Hellcats took off and began to head west to meet the incoming Japanese aircraft. The Hellcats met the raid at 10:25am, approximately 54 miles west of the task force and began to destroy it.

By 10:48am the massive dogfight of milling aircraft had reached the battleship formation, and Lee's ships put up a barrage of AA fire. The CAP, together with the volume of battleship AA fire, prevented any large air attack being made against Lee's battleships, or continuing through to the carriers. *Indiana* had the first success in downing an aircraft, but at 10:49am *South Dakota* suffered a direct hit from a 500lb bomb on the port side of her superstructure, killing 24 and wounding 27. By 10:57am the air-sea battle was over, but a second wave of 128 Japanese aircraft was heading toward the fleet.

Between 11:50am and 12:15am, dive and torpedo bombers attacked Lee's battleships, but the volume of AA fire prevented any aircraft from completing their attack. At 12:14pm, *Indiana* had a Japanese torpedo plane crash into and bounce off its starboard quarter at the waterline which dented, but did not rupture, the outer plating of the ship's hull. *Indiana* shot down five aircraft. Fast battleships accounted for nine aircraft downed in what came to be known as the "Marianas Turkey shoot" as Japan lost

Damage to the port secondary battery director caused by friendly fire.

244 carrier aircraft. The combination of the Hellcat, aggressive fighter pilots, and excellent vectoring by fighter direction resulted in an overwhelming victory for the Fifth Fleet. However, six of the nine Japanese carriers survived the battle and were to play a critical role in the battle of Leyte Gulf.

South China Sea

During the night of January 10, 1945, *North Carolina*, *Washington*, *South Dakota*, and *Massachusetts*, as part of Admiral Halsey's Third Fleet, steamed into the South China Sea, the heart of Japan's supply route from the oil fields of South Asia to Japan. US submarines had practically cut this route, so that the remaining heavy units of the IJN had to be stationed near the oil source rather than in Japanese harbors. Admiral Halsey's objectives were to seek out the IJN, sink merchant shipping, and destroy aircraft located on the Indo and South China coast and Formosa (modern Taiwan). By the time Halsey's fleet reached the IJN anchorage at Camranh

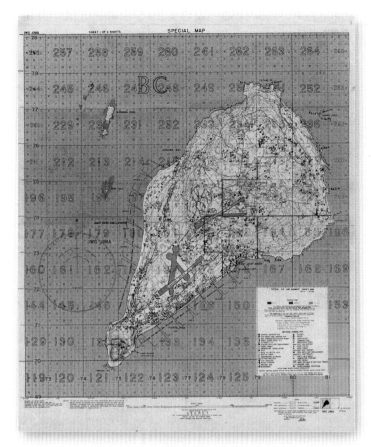

The gunnery target map for the bombardment of Iwo Jima.

Bay, the IJN ships had withdrawn to Singapore. Aircraft from the Third Fleet destroyed over 100 aircraft along the Indo-China coast, Hainan, Formosa, and Hong Kong. Twelve oil tankers were sunk plus 32 other merchant ships and two IJN vessels. During this operation, the fast battleships refueled destroyers two at a time. The Third Fleet returned to the Pacific on January 20 without sustaining any damage.

Shore bombardment

Fast battleships were used for pre-invasion bombardment of Japanese-held Pacific Islands, with the carriers providing air cover. In a number of instances, Saipan, Tinian, and Iwo Jima, the shore bombardment was a significant disappointment, as many targets were not destroyed. The accuracy required to hit pill-boxes defending beaches and command posts was almost impossible to achieve given the trajectory of 16-inch shells.

Shore bombardment required a different approach to ship-vs-ship gunfire. Main plot, the ship's navigator, and the crew of the Kingfisher spotting aircraft required an accurate navigational chart showing the ship's planned track and the target area on land. The target area was overlaid with a grid and numbered to provide coordinates in order to fix a target's position, which included its elevation above sea level. The ship had to be navigated precisely, allowing for current and wind effect on the ship's position, which then had to be determined every few minutes. The range and bearing to the target was calculated on the chart, and provided the input for the Range Keeper, rather than from the directors and radar plot. This system did not allow for rapid and continuous fire. However, against large industrial plants near

 CAMOUFLAGE SCHEMES 1944–47

Towards the end of the war, the *North Carolina* underwent further changes to her camouflage scheme.

1. Designed to fool surface observers with the impression of greater distance provided by its false horizon effect, the Measure 22 graded system was widely applied to US Navy vessels in the Atlantic and European coastal waters from late 1942, and in the Pacific from late 1944. *North Carolina* bore this pattern from 1945 to 1946. The scheme comprised navy blue on the hull horizontal to the lower point of sheer, haze gray on all vertical surfaces above this point, and deck blue on all decks.

2. In 1947, the *North Carolina* adopted the Measure 13 haze gray system, which saw the ship repainted entirely in haze gray, save for the traditional deck blue, which was used on all decking. This pattern was thought to provide reasonable protection under a variety of situations, and was adopted widely by ships in the post-war years.

1

2

Washington leads *North Carolina*, and *South Dakota* as they follow USS *Ticonderoga* in the South China Sea, January 1945.

the coast of Japan, which could be spotted by director and located by radar as well as the bombardment chart, battleship gunfire was devastating. On August 9, 1945, firing on and destroying the iron and steel center at Kamaishi, *Massachusetts*, which had fired the first 16-inch shell for the US Navy in World War II, fired the last 16-inch shell of that war.

CONCLUSION

The loss of the pre-1922 battleships at Pearl Harbor put the new fast battleships along with carriers into the front line of the Pacific war. It is ironic that the role of fast battleships in the Pacific, as part of fast carrier task forces, was the one rejected by the General Board of the US Navy when their design was finalized. As fast battleships, the North Carolina and South Dakota class were not fast enough, with a top speed deficit of 6 knots compared to carriers.

However, the secondary armament of quick-firing, high-angle 20 5-inch/38 guns and range were powerful enough to break up dive and torpedo bombers attacking carriers, even as the carriers steamed away from the battleships. The fact that the US Navy did not lose one carrier escorted by a fast battleship to air attack, after losing three unescorted by October 1942, is telling.

In the only fast battleship versus fast battleship action at sea, *Washington*'s battle with *Kirishima* showed the destructive capability of the combination of 16-inch guns and armor-piercing shells married to fire-control radar,

BELOW
Massachusetts leads *South Dakota* and *Indiana* and a heavy cruiser prior to bombarding the Iron Works at Kamaishi, Honshu, in July 1945.

BELOW RIGHT
North Carolina bombards the Japanese mainland. Three 16-inch shells can be seen in the upper left of the picture.

the Ford Range Keeper, directors, and a highly trained crew. Firing 75 shells in five and a half minutes at *Kirishima*, which was approaching on an opposing course, with *Washington*'s gun turrets training at 20 degrees per minute, a closing speed of 54 knots, with a rapid change of course by *Kirishima*, all at night and achieving a minimum accuracy rate of 12 percent, makes this action by *Washington* the most effective example of accurate battleship gunfire in battleship history for the period 1905–45.

In addition to the fast battleships' strong main and AA armament, their fuel and stores capacity, cruising range, and ability to refuel destroyers multiplied their lethal capability. From their entry into the Atlantic and Pacific theaters until the end of the war, these ships were able to sustain a high level of operational performance, demonstrating the quality of their machinery and equipment, together with the operating efficiency and stamina of their crews.

War's end, homeward bound. *North Carolina* transits the Panama Canal, October 1945.

The only demonstrated vulnerability of fast battleships was the command and control structure of the bridge and superstructure tower, located above the armored deck, as shown by *South Dakota* during the night battle of Guadalcanal.

The unanswered question regarding these ships is how they would have performed in action against the *Musashi* and *Yamato*, when on the receiving end of 18-inch shells. Fortunately, the bravery and skill of US carrier aircrews makes this question purely academic.

The battles of the Eastern Solomons and Santa Cruz during the Guadalcanal campaign, involving the *North Carolina* and *South Dakota* respectively, established a new primary role for the six battleships as close-in escorts to US fast carriers. This melding of mutually supporting ships into task forces, whereby no carriers nor battleships escorting each other were sunk by enemy bombs or torpedoes, created a new weapon system for the US Navy which then drove across the Pacific from Pearl Harbor to Tokyo Bay and took care of the Kongo fast battleships as well as the *Musashi* and *Yamato* in the process.

Three fast battleships, the *North Carolina*, *Alabama*, and *Massachusetts*, have survived as memorials and museums, so it is still possible to walk along the sweeping weather deck from bow to stern, climb into a 16-inch gun turret and grip the trigger mechanism, wander through a maze of compartments,

North Carolina and *Washington* in formation during the summer midshipman cruise from Annapolis.

Battleship *North Carolina* today as a museum in Wilmington, North Carolina.

twirl the handles on the Ford Range Keeper, study a radar plot, look at an amazing range of dials and levers in a machinery room, hold the helm in the conning tower behind 16 inches of armor, look into a 5-inch gun turret, sit behind a 40mm Bofors gun and then stand behind a 20mm gun on an open deck and gaze out and imagine an attacking aircraft.

BIBLIOGRAPHY

Books

There is a wealth of books on battleships and the naval war in the Pacific. The author found the following to be helpful:

Blee, Captain Ben, USN, *Battleship North Carolina* (Battleship North Carolina)

Felker, Craig C., *Testing American Sea Power: US Navy Strategic Exercises, 1923–1940*

Friedman, Norman, *US Battleships* (Naval Institute Press)

Friedman, Norman, *Naval Firepower* (Naval Institute Press)

Garzke/Dulin, *Battleships: United States Battleships 1935–1992* (Naval Institute Press)

Glover, Admiral Cato D., USN, *Command Performance with Guts* (Greenwich Book Publishers)

Kuehn, John T., *Agents of Innovation: The General Board and the Design of the Fleet that Defeated the Japanese Navy* (Naval Institute Press)

Naval Historical Center, *Operational Experience of Fast Battleships* (Department of the Navy)

Smith, Douglas V., *Carrier Battles: Command Decisions in Harm's Way* (Naval Institute Press)

Wildenberg, Thomas, *All the Factors of Victory* (Brassey's Inc)

Internet

www.battleshipnc.com

www.ussalabama.com

www.battleshipcove.org/bb59-history.htm

www.hnsa.org

APPENDICES

North Carolina class

	North Carolina (BB-55)	*Washington* (BB-56)
Builder	New York Navy Yard, Brooklyn, NY	Philadelphia Navy Yard, Philadelphia, PA
Laid down	October 27, 1937	June 14, 1938
Launched	June 13, 1940	June 1, 1940
Commissioned	April 9, 1941	May 15, 1941
Disposition	Dedicated as a war memorial at Wilmington, NC, on October 3, 1961	Scrapped 1961
Displacement	(1942) 36,600 tons Standard, 44,800 tons Full load (1945) 46,700 tons Full load	(1942) 36,600 tons Standard, 44,800 tons Full load (1945) 45,370 tons Full load
Dimensions	728'8" Length overall 713'5" Waterline length 108'3" Maximum beam 104'6" Waterline beam 31'7" Mean draft 35'6" Maximum draft	728'11" Length overall 713'8" Waterline length 108'3" Maximum beam 104'6" Waterline beam 31'8" Mean draft 34'9" Maximum draft

Armament

	North Carolina (BB-55)	*Washington* (BB-56)
Main	Nine 16-inch/45 caliber guns (Mark 6)	Nine 16-inch/45 caliber guns (Mark 6)
Secondary	Twenty 5-inch/38 caliber guns (Mark 12)	Twenty 5-inch/38 caliber guns (Mark 12)

Anti-aircraft

	40mm	1.1"	20mm	.50 cal		40mm	1.1"	20mm	.50 cal
Apr 1941	none	16	none	12	Apr 1941	none	16	none	12
Dec 1941	none	16	40	12	Dec 1941	none	16	20	12
June 1942	none	16	40	28	June 1942	none	16	20	28
Dec 1944	60	none	48	none	Dec 1944	60	none	67	none
June 1945	60	none	36	none	Aug 1945	60	none	83	none
					Nov 1945	60	none	63	none

Armor

	North Carolina (BB-55)	*Washington* (BB-56)
Belt armor	12" inclined 15° Tapered to 6.6"	12" inclined 15° Tapered to 6.6"
Deck armor		
Main	1.45"	1.45"
Second	1.4" + 3.6"	1.4" + 3.6"
Third	0.62"	0.62"
Total	**7.07"**	**7.07"**
Barbette armor		
Centerline forward	14.7"	14.7"
Sides	16.0"	16.0"
Centerline aft	11.5"	11.5"
Turret armor		
Face plates	16.0"	16.0"
Sides	9.8"	9.8"
Back plates	11.8"	11.8"
Roof plates	7.0"	7.0"
Secondary gun armor		
Gun mounts	1.95"	1.95"
Magazines	1.95"	1.95"
Conning tower armor		
Centerline sides	14.7"	14.7"
Beam sides	16.0"	16.0"
Roof plates	7.0"	7.0"
Comm. tube	14.0"	14.0"

Machinery

	North Carolina (BB-55)	*Washington* (BB-56)
Boiler	Eight Babcock & Wilcox three drum boilers fitted with two furnaces and double uptakes. Pressure: 575 psi. Temperature: 850°F	Eight Babcock & Wilcox three drum boilers fitted with two furnaces and double uptakes. Pressure: 575 psi. Temperature: 850°F
Turbines	Four sets General Electric geared turbines High pressure impulse turbines – 12 stages, 5,904 rpm maximum Low pressure impulse turbines – 6 stages, 4,937 rpm maximum Astern impulse turbines – 3 stages, 3,299 rpm maximum	Four sets General Electric geared turbines High pressure impulse turbines – 12 stages, 5,904 rpm maximum Low pressure impulse turbines – 6 stages, 4,937 rpm maximum Astern impulse turbines – 3 stages, 3,299 rpm maximum
Shaft horsepower	121,000 (32,000 astern)	121,000 (32,000 astern)
Maximum speed	28.0 knots @ 199 rpm and 121,000 shp – 1941 26.8 knots – 1945	28.0 knots @ 199 rpm and 121,000 shp – 1941 26.8 knots – 1945
Nominal endurance	17,450 nautical miles @ 15 knots – 1941 16,320 nautical miles @ 15 knots – 1945 5,740 nautical miles @ 25 knots – 1945	17,450 nautical miles @ 15 knots – 1941 16,320 nautical miles @ 15 knots – 1945 5,740 nautical miles @ 25 knots – 1945
Generators	Four ship's service turbogenerators (1.250kw) Four ship's service diesel generators (850kw) Two emergency diesel generators (200kw)	Four ship's service turbogenerators (1.250kw) Four ship's service diesel generators (850kw) Two emergency diesel generators (200kw)

South Dakota class

	South Dakota (BB-57)	Indiana (BB-58)
Builder	New York Shipbuilding Corp., Camden, NJ	Newport News Shipbuilding & Dry Dock Co., Newport News, VA
Laid down	July 5, 1939	November 20, 1939
Launched	June 7, 1941	November 21, 1941
Commissioned	March 20, 1942	April 30, 1942
Disposition	Scrapped 1962 Parts to South Dakota for war memorial	Scrapped 1961
Displacement	(1942) 38,664 tons Standard 44,519 tons Full load (1945) 38,506 tons Standard 46,200 tons Full load	(1942) 44,374 tons Full load (1945) 35,900 tons Standard 44,600 tons Full load
Dimensions	680'4" Length overall 666'0" Waterline length 108'1" Maximum beam 27'9" Mean draft 36'4" Maximum draft	680'0" Length overall 666'0" Waterline length 108'2" Maximum beam 27'9" Mean draft 36'2" Maximum draft

Armament

	South Dakota (BB-57)	Indiana (BB-58)
Main	Nine 16-inch/45 caliber guns (Mark 6)	Nine 16-inch/45 caliber guns (Mark 6)
Secondary	Sixteen 5-inch/38 caliber guns (Mark 12)	Twenty 5-inch/38 caliber guns (Mark 12)

Anti-aircraft

	40mm	1.1"	20mm	.50 cal
Mar 1942	none	28	16	8
Sept 1942	16	20	36	none
Feb 1943	68	none	35	none
Dec 1944	68	none	72	none
Mar 1945	68	none	77	none

	40mm	1.1"	20mm	.50 cal
June 1942	24	none	16	none
Dec 1944	48	none	55	none
Dec 1945	48	none	52	none

Armor

	South Dakota (BB-57)	Indiana (BB-58)
Belt armor	12.2" inclined 19°	12.2" inclined 19°
Lower belt armor	12.2" tapered to 1.0"	12.2" tapered to 1.0"
Deck armor		
Main	1.5"	1.5"
Second	5.0" + 0.75"	5.0" + 0.75"
Splinter	0.625"	0.625"
Third	0.3"	0.3"
Total	**8.175"**	**8.175"**
Barbette armor		
Centerline	11.6"	11.6"
Sides	17.3"	17.3"
Turret armor		
Face plates	18.0"	18.0"
Sides	9.5"	9.5"
Back plates	12.0"	12.0"
Roof plates	7.25"	7.25"
Secondary gun armor		
Gun mounts	2.0"	2.0"
Magazines	2.0"	2.0"
Conning tower armor		
Sides	16.0"	16.0"
Roof plates	7.25"	7.25"
Bottom plates	4.0"	4.0"
Comm. tube	16.0"	16.0"

Machinery

	South Dakota (BB-57)	Indiana (BB-58)
Boiler	Eight Babcock & Wilcox three drum boilers fitted with two furnaces and double uptakes Pressure: 578 psi Temperature: 850°F	Eight Foster Wheeler three drum boilers fitted with two furnaces and double uptakes Pressure: 578 psi Temperature: 850°F
Turbines	Four sets General Electric geared turbines	Four sets Westinghouse geared turbines
Shaft horsepower	130,000 (32,000 astern)	130,000 (32,000 astern)
Maximum speed	27.8 knots @ 185 rpm – 1941 27.0 knots – 1945	27.8 knots @ 185 rpm – 1941 27.0 knots – 1945
Nominal endurance	17,000 nautical miles @ 15 knots – 1945 6,400 nautical miles @ 25 knots – 1945	17,000 nautical miles @ 15 knots – 1945 6,400 nautical miles @ 25 knots – 1945
Generators	Seven ship's service turbogenerators (1,000kw) Two emergency diesel generators (200kw)	Seven ship's service turbogenerators (1,000kw) Two emergency diesel generators (200kw)

	Massachusetts (BB-59)	*Alabama* (BB-60)
Builder	Bethlehem Steel Co., Quincy, MA	Norfolk Navy Yard, Portsmouth, VA
Laid down	July 20, 1939	February 1, 1940
Launched	September 23, 1941	February 16, 1942
Commissioned	May 12, 1942	August 16, 1942
Disposition	Dedicated as a war memorial at Fall River, MA, on June 12, 1965	Dedicated as a war memorial at Mobile, AL, in 1964
Displacement	(1942) 45,216 tons Full load (1945) 38,988 tons Standard 46,314 tons Full load	(1942) 44,800 tons Full load
Dimensions	680'9" Length overall 666'0" Waterline length 108'2" Maximum beam 28'7" Mean draft 36'9" Maximum draft	679'5" Length overall 666'0" Waterline length 108'1" Maximum beam 28'4" Mean draft 36'2" Maximum draft

Armament

	Massachusetts (BB-59)	*Alabama* (BB-60)
Main	Nine 16-inch/45 caliber guns (Mark 6)	Nine 16-inch/45 caliber guns (Mark 6)
Secondary	Twenty 5-inch/38 caliber guns (Mark 12)	Twenty 5-inch/38 caliber guns (Mark 12)

Anti-aircraft

	40mm	1.1"	20mm	.50 cal		40mm	1.1"	20mm	.50 cal
May 1942	24	none	35	none	Aug 1942	24	none	22	none
Dec 1944	72	none	38	none	Dec 1944	48	none	52	none
June 1945	72	none	33	none	Feb 1945	48	none	56	none
Nov 1945	72	none	41	none	Nov 1945	48	none	52	none

Armor

	Massachusetts (BB-59)	*Alabama* (BB-60)
Belt armor	12.2" inclined 19°	12.2" inclined 19°
Lower belt armor	12.2" tapered to 1.0"	12.2" tapered to 1.0"
Deck armor		
Main	1.5"	1.5"
Second	5.0" + 0.75"	5.0" + 0.75"
Splinter	0.625"	0.625"
Third	0.3"	0.3"
Total	**8.175"**	**8.175"**
Barbette armor		
Centerline	11.6"	11.6"
Sides	17.3"	17.3"
Turret armor		
Face plates	18.0"	18.0"
Sides	9.5"	9.5"
Back plates	12.0"	12.0"
Roof plates	7.25"	7.25"
Secondary gun armor		
Gun mounts	2.0"	2.0"
Magazines	2.0"	2.0"
Conning tower armor		
Sides	16.0"	16.0"
Roof plates	7.25"	7.25"
Bottom plates	4.0"	4.0"
Comm. tube	16.0"	16.0"

Machinery

	Massachusetts (BB-59)	*Alabama* (BB-60)
Boiler	Eight Babcock & Wilcox three drum boilers fitted with two furnaces and double uptakes Pressure: 578 psi Temperature: 850°F	Eight Foster Wheeler three drum boilers fitted with two furnaces and double uptakes Pressure: 578 psi Temperature: 850°F
Turbines	Four sets General Electric geared turbines	Four sets Westinghouse geared turbines
Shaft horsepower	130,000 (32,000 astern)	130,000 (32,000 astern)
Maximum speed	27.8 knots @ 185 rpm – 1941 27.0 knots – 1945	27.8 knots @ 185 rpm – 1941 27.0 knots – 1945
Nominal endurance	17,000 nautical miles @ 15 knots – 1945 6,400 nautical miles @ 25 knots – 1945	17,000 nautical miles @ 15 knots – 1945 6,400 nautical miles @ 25 knots – 1945
Generators	Seven ship's service turbogenerators (1,000kw) Two emergency diesel generators (200kw)	Seven ship's service turbogenerators (1,000kw) Two emergency diesel generators (200kw)

INDEX

Note: letters in **bold** refer to plates and illustrations.